Isle of Iona

By

E. RAYMOND CAPT, M.A., A.I.A., F.S.A. Scot.

Iona Abbey

Copyright © 2003 by Artisan Publishers

All Rights Reserved

ISBN: 0-934666-58-X

IONA

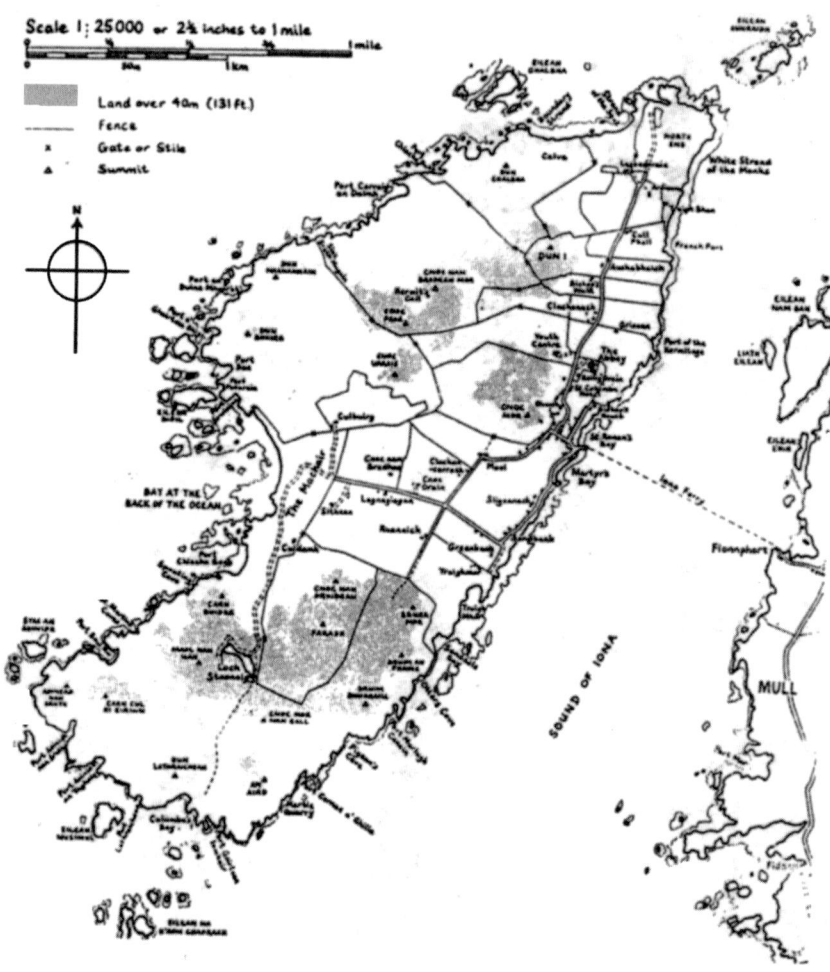

CONTENTS

	Page
Preface	5
The Island	7
St. Columba in Ireland	13
The Arrival of Columba on Iona	27
The Iona Community	33
The Iona Scribes	41
The Death of St. Columba	51
Columba the King Maker	57
Columba the Missionary	66
Later History of Iona	72
The Culdee Church	76
Iona Monastery (Abbey) Today	84
The Crosses of Iona	112
Flowers of Iona	130
Prophecy of St. Columba	142
Celtic Songs and Poems	146
Conclusion	154
Notable Dates - History of Iona	156

PREFACE

Very few people are familiar with the name Iona, but once it was one of the best loved names in Christendom. It is a little island in the midst of the Inner Hebrides or Western Islands of Scotland. Its ancient name in Gaelic (or Pictish) was "Ious" and it was also known by the name "Innis-nam-Druidbneach" or Island of the Druids. It is possible that the name Iona is derived from "Ee-hona" (L-shona) meaning blessed or Sacred Isle. We know the Norsemen called Iona the Holy Island.

It is noteworthy that the Hebrew word for Dove is Iona, and in Latin, Columbia, for under the influence of a man by the name of St. Columba, the glory and renown of Iona blossomed into full glory. It developed into the most famous center of Celtic Culdee Christianity, the mother community from whence missionaries were dispatched for the conversion of the pagan tribes in Scotland and Northern England.

Iona played an important part in the founding of the Scottish nation. It was on Iona that Columba crowned Aidan (son of Gabran the king of Dalriada) King of Scotland, upon the stone Lia Fail, the Stone upon which the Patriarch Jacob rested his head the night he dreamed of a ladder stretching to heaven with God at the top. For centuries this Stone sat under the Coronation Chair in Westminster Abbey in London. In 1999 the Stone was moved to Edinburgh Castle in Scotland.

It has been said of Iona, "Blessed is the eye that see-eth it, especially in the spring and summer months." So very small and modest in its aspects and overshadowed by its more imposing sister island, Iona sacred spell is often missed by the passing stranger. But for those who have eyes to see there is a subtle beauty in its apparent barrenness: a beauty of atmosphere; a beauty part physical and part spiritual.

This book is dedicated to my wife, Janice Roseanne Capt (1924-1987), who accompanied me three times to this tiny beautiful island. She joins me in spirit to welcome you to the story of "The Isle of Iona."

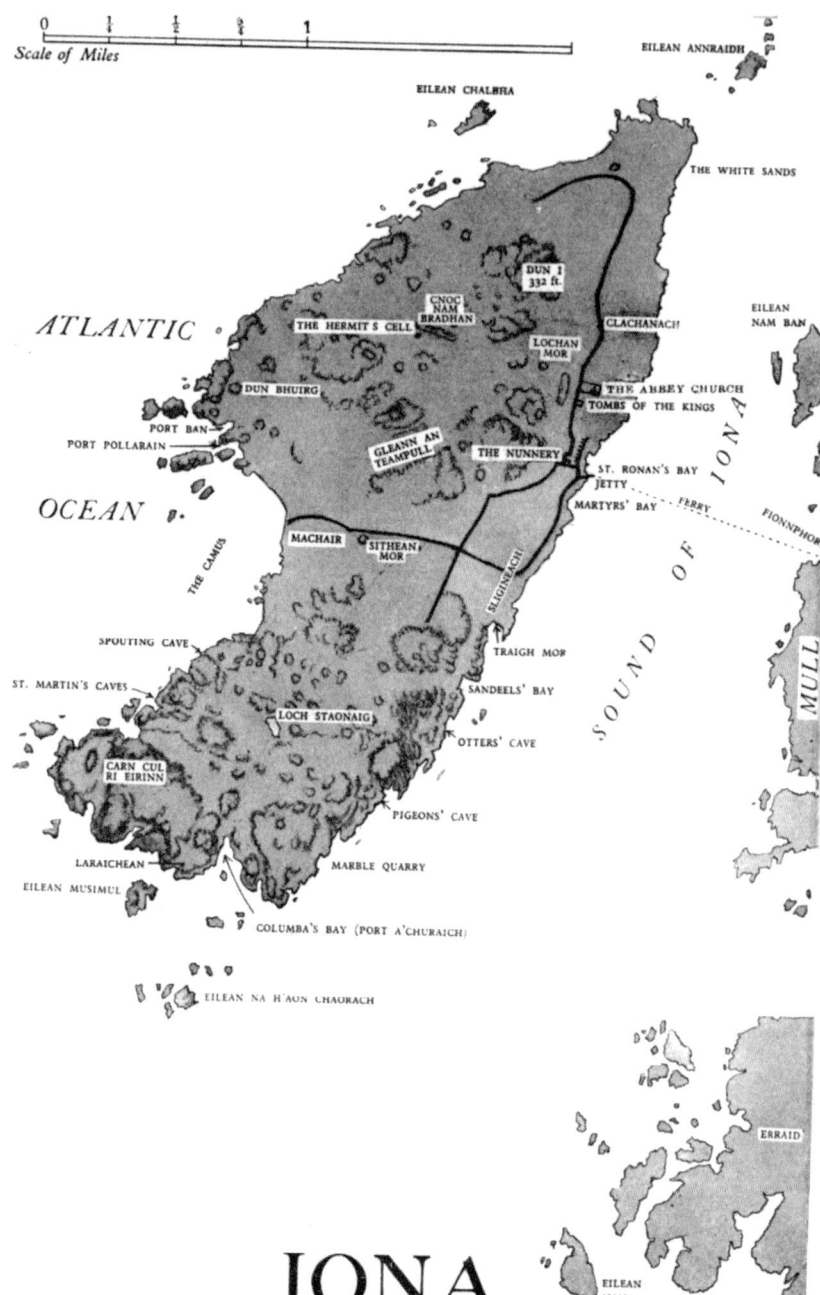

THE ISLAND

Iona is a very small island lying within the Inner Hebrides, about three miles long and one and a half miles wide. Its area thus being about twenty-two hundred acres. It is low lying, its highest elevation, Dun I (Dun-ee) is under four hundred feet. For its size, Iona contains much variety of features. A belt of arable land crosses the middle of the island, and a tract of it lies to the north of the present abbey. Elsewhere, among the crags and heather, the great-horned, shaggy Highland cattle find excellent pasturage. To the south lie stretches of boggy moorland, and on the heights are rock "that wade in heather and upon whose brows the sea-wind waves the yellow lichen." (Fiona MacLeod).

The landscape of Iona is treeless, though a few small trees have been reared in gardens, but there is a wonderful variety of wild flowers scenting the air with a pleasing fragrance. A favorite flower of the inhabitants of Iona is the little yellow St. John's Wort (Hvpericum), owing perhaps to its shape, which suggests a cross. The much admired (usually from a distance) Scot's Thistle, adds to the colorful landscape. It is the national emblem of Scotland. According to tradition, the Danes came upon the Scots unperceived in the dead of night. But one of them chanced to step on a thistle and the resulting loud cry of pain awoke the unsuspecting Scots, who at once attacked the invaders and gained a complete victory.

There are various land-birds on Iona, but the cliff and sea-birds predominate. These include the beautiful oyster-catcher, named in Gaelic, "Gille-brigde". In modern times snow-white pigeons were introduced to the island. Fish abound in the waters around Iona and seals are often found on the lonelier beaches. There are no snakes on the island, though they are plentiful just across the Sound on the island of Mull. Tradition credits Columba with the immunity of the island in this respect, but a more modern explanation is the quality of the soil.

Once Iona stood alone in the vastness of the water, mute and desolate. The solitude broken only by the Atlantic seas that beat ceaselessly against its upward reaching rocks. Today, however, the Hebridean seas which surround Iona are island studded to a far horizon. Separated, yet dwarfed by its younger sister islands, it enjoys a mildness of climate and a natural fertility favorable to cultivation.

One and a quarter miles to the east of Iona is the Ross, or Isle of Mull, with its misty mountains and shadowy glens, once stirring with human life, but now mostly the home of the red deer. To the northwest are the rocky Treshnish Islands of Staffa, with its great cathedral caves created by the action of the waves and the weather throughout the centuries. The largest of the caves is Fingal's Cave and the most visited today. Its old name is "Uamb Bhinn", the Melodious Cavern.

The height of the great arch of the cavern is sixty-two feet (at mean tide) and the depth of the sea below is about the same. The cliff above rises a further thirty feet and its length is about two hundred and twenty-seven feet. The sides of the cave, at the entrance, are vertical and nearly parallel, and are composed of black basaltic pillars, of which the majority are pentagonal or hexagonal in form. They are divided transversal by joints, like the columns of ancient Greek temples.

A constant boom, as of distant thunder, fills the air as the Atlantic waves burst into the cave, and the voices of the sea-birds ring high and clear above the tumult. Sir Robert Peel (British Statesman 1788-1850) after a visit to Staffa wrote: "I have seen the temple not made with hands and have felt the majestic swell of the ocean - the pulsation of the great Atlantic - beating in its inmost sanctuary, and pealing a note of praise nobler far than any that ever pealed from human organ."

Mendelssohn's famous "Fengal's Cave" overture was composed after a visit to the cave by the composer. It is here that Mendelssohn, when returning to the mainland, immediately made for the piano in the home where he was lodging to try out the theme that had been inspired by his excursion to the cave. He had hardly laid a finger on the keys when he was brusquely interrupted by his Scottish host who reminded him that it was Sunday and therefore music was out of the question. When Brahms heard the finished overture he is reported to have said, "I would sacrifice all my works to have been able to compose an overture like it."

Further off north of Iona lies the long low island of Tiree, once cultivated by the early inhabitants of Iona when the island could no longer support the growing community. West of Iona, beyond the tiny Calf Island close by, where seals were raised for food and skins, the vast Atlantic sea stretches for 2000 miles in an unbroken sweep to the shores of Labrador.

The village of Iona consists of a single street on the eastern side of the island. From the village a single road leads inland, linking several small farms. The modern population of the island averages around two hundred permanent residents. Fishing, agriculture and raising sheep and cattle are the main occupations of the island. In the winter months the spinning-wheel hums by the fireside preparing the sheep's wool, carted, and dyed with roots and sea-weeds for weaving on hand-looms, being carried out by the island craftsfolk. Some of the inhabitants augment their income by providing lodging for visitors to the island during the summer months.

The Village, Iona.

Regular visitors to Iona travel through Mull by car or coach and cross the Sound of Iona by ferry from Fionnphort. Many other visitors come by steamer from Oban on the west coast of Scotland and are ferried by small boats to the quay at Iona. The village of Iona starts from the quay and consists of a single street on the eastern side of the island. From the village a single street leads inland, linking several small farms. The modern population of the island averages around two hundred permanent residents. Winter gales can sometimes cut the island off for days.

Geologically speaking, the Isle of Iona is not only immeasurably older than its sister islands, but also than the highest mountains and most of the dry land on the earth. The surrounding islands were formed many ages later than Iona. During the great earth-changes of the

Tertiary Period (between 15 and 30 million years ago) the face of the globe attained, with minor differences, its present configuration. At that time an enormous plain of hardened lava burst out of the earth in a molten eruption. The granite of the island of Mull, the basalt of Staffa and the Treshnish Islands, are all that is left above water of that gigantic eruption. The rest has been broken up and engulfed by the devouring sea.

However, of Iona it can be said, its beginning is almost a part of the beginning of the world itself. Our earth had its beginning as a flaming mass of combustion, like a sun, but over two billion years ago, began to cool and shrivel into a globe with a solid crust. This primitive crust was composed of cooled lava, granite and other rocks of glassy or crystalline texture, which we term igneous rocks. These rocks contained no fossils, for so far as it is known, no living creatures as yet existed on this primeval land.

As the first oceans condensed in the hollows of its surface, rains began to form and start its processes of erosion of the high places. As the rains increased, great beds of sediments were laid down in the ocean floors. These early beds, under pressure from overlying beds and heat from the earth's core, became hard, rugged and twisted. It was of these Achaean rocks, developed on the sea-bottom, from which Iona and the Outer Hebrides Islands were formed.

Pushed up by the sea and by the then still convulsing earth, these rocks give evidence of the vast heat and pressure they have undergone. A product of such conditions is marble, and on the south side of Iona can be seen huge dikes or veins of greenish-white marble. Above the cliffs in the granite dikes one can readily see the resulting flowing and folding of the rock strata under the great heat and pressure.

June is the most lovely month of the whole year to visit Iona, for then darkness hardly falls at all. On a clear summer day, and particularly when the wind is in the north, the beauty of Iona is idyllic. Soft cirrus clouds veil the blue vault of heaven. Over the wide dazzling sands the sea glistens green as an emerald while further out it is of vivid blue, barred with purple. The granite cliffs of the nearby island of Mull glow rosy across the Sound and the great mountains beyond cast their deep-blue shadow on the still waters.

Those who enjoy the beauty of sea and sky, of a landscape tinted with sunrise, will experience the beauty of Iona as Columba saw it. He walked the same pastures, stood on the same pure white sands (formed of the crushed shells of small land-snails) and knew he lived very close to God, the Creator of all beauty. To his God, he intoned his Sea-Prayer as he stood on the shore praying for the safe return of one of his monks he had sent on an errand.

"At mouth of day
The hour of birds
Stood Columba
On the great White strand:
'O King of Storms.
Home sail the boat
From far away:
Thou King on High,
Home sail the boat!"

ST. COLUMBA IN IRELAND

St. Columba, or Columcille, was born in the year A.D. 521 at Gartan, a wild and remote district of Donegal, Ireland. His father, Phelim MacFergus, king and chieftain of that district, belonged to the clan of the Cinel Conaill, descendants of Niall of the Nine Hostages. Niall was the traditional founder of the so-called High Kings of Ireland (the Celtic kings who ruled from Tara) who reigned at the time when St. Patrick (born about A.D. 389) was brought over as a slave-boy of thirteen from Britain. Columba's mother, Eithne, belonged to the Royal House of Leister and his grandmother, Erea, (daughter of King Erc) was a sister of Fergus Mor McErc (the Great). Thus Columba belonged to the royal of Ireland.

A prophecy by St. Patrick of the birth of a famous man of the race of Niall has been ascribed to Columba:

>A man-child shall be born of his family,
>He will be a sage, a prophet, a poet,
>A loveable lamp, pure and clear,
>Who will not utter falsehoods.
>He will be a sage, he will be pious,
>He will be the King of the royal graces,
>He will be lasting and will be ever good,
>He will be in the eternal kingdom for his consolation.

Columba was baptized "Colum" meaning "Dove", or in Latin "Columba" to which was afterwards add the suffix, "cille" as some say from his close attendance at church. Tradition has that he was given a second name "Crimthann", meaning fox or wolf. As a boy, Columba had no interest in the princely living his royal station would have afforded him. Instead he aspired toward a more spiritual life. To this end he spent much time in solitude and study of the Scriptures. He had a great love of the land and of wild nature, and the countryside was for the most part his home.

Much of what we know of the life of St. Columba comes from the writings of the Irish historian, Adamnan (or Adomnan) who lived between A.D. 624 and 704. Adamnan was a direct descendant from Fergus, son of Conall Guiban and therefore from Columba's grandfather. Adamnan belonged to the same Scottish tribe as Columba and later went as a young man to Columba's monastery at Iona, where he lived with the brethren trained by Columba himself. In A.D. when Adamnan was fifty years of age he was elected Abbot of Hy (Iona) and became the ninth Abbot in succession from the founder, St. Columba.

Because Adamnan thought in Gaelic and wrote in Latin, some scholars state that his style of writing is difficult. However, his biography "The Life of St. Columkille," written about one hundred years after the Saint's death in A.D. 579 "is considered the most complete piece of biography that all Europe can boast of, not only at so early a period but throughout the Middle Ages" (Pinkerton). It became the standard class book in the monasteries of England and Wales. Wandering scholars took scraps of the book to the Continent.

Adamnan compiled a record of the Saint's life from oral and written sources. The oral authorities, Adamnan assured his readers, were chosen from among a great many for their reliability, so far as that could be ascertained. We must bear in mind that Adamnan's purpose was not primarily history but edification, and history was of importance chiefly as a means to this end, not an end in itself. He sought to present us with a picture of the Saint's personality and mission; a true picture of Columba as he believed the Saint to have been.

Adamnan's narrative is however, consistent with the conditions prevalent in the fifth century and avoids the error of ascribing to Columba developments which took place in his Church at a later day, such as territorial expansion, numerous new foundations and the development of scholarships and extensive secular studies. The Saint whom Adamnan has pictured for us is an Abbot devoted to the community among whom he lived and to the services of its church, and to his own spiritual life. He pictures him as a student devoted to the study of the Scriptures. Yet in fact some incidents in his history suggests the active life of an influential diplomat.

As a young man Columba received a religious education. When he was old enough he was sent to the monastic school of Moville (in County Down) under the tutorage of the famous scholar St. Finian or Finbar (white-head). St. Finian had been trained at Candida Casa (white house), the first Christian settlement in what is now Scotland. Candida Casa was founded by St. Finian, the apostle of the northern Britons and the Picks at Whithorn in Galloway, in the year 397 while southern Britain was still a Roman province.

St. Finian took special delight with his dedicated pupil. Although little is known about Columba's life at Moville, it is recorded he was ordained a deacon before he left to study under a Christian bard called Gemman. As a student under Gemman, Columba studied music, literature and Greek grammar. (Amra Choluimbchille, Vol. XX, page 405). The bards of ancient Ireland were learned men in all the arts and classics including philosophy, literature, divinity, and such sciences as was then known. Latin was not then a dead language, but was spoken in the schools along with Greek.

Columba received his final schooling at the famous ecclesiastical house at Clonard under the direction of another St. Finian, one of the succession of Irish scholars who made Ireland famous all over Europe. Clonard was then the most distinguished school which Ireland possessed and gathered students from every part of the civilized world. Archbishop Ussher (1581-1656) writes in his "Antiquitates Ecclesiarum Britannicarum":

"From the school of Clonard, scholars of old came out in great numbers as Greeks from the side of the horse of Troy. The usual number of pupils in attendance is set down at three thousand, so that ancient analysts call St. Finian himself 'a doctor of wisdom, and tutor of the saints of Ireland in his time,' while from the fact that he taught St. Columba, Kieran of Conmacnois, Brendan of Confert, and a number of other celebrated bishops and abbots, he was styled preceptor of the twelve apostles of Ireland."

Columba helped Finian with the services of the church and transcribing the sacred books, one of the chief occupations of the monks. There were few copies of the Scriptures in those days, and one of the duties of the monastic schools was to multiply them in order that each church might have its own copy. For much as Columba loved the work of a scribe, he desired active missionary work; to found new monasteries and churches and to encourage those which already existed. He also wanted to become involved in the national and political affairs of his day.

About the age of twenty-five Columba renounced all claim of the right of succession to the kingship of Erin, for God. He was ordained to

Ireland in Columba's Time

the priesthood. After a short sojourn at the monastery Glasnevin, on the River Finglass near Dublin, Columba migrated to his ancestral home in Ulster. There at Derry, (the place of the oaks) within thirty miles of his birthplace, he planted his first monastery (A.D. 546) on ground given to him by his own tribe, the Clan Niall.

Derry monastery lay on rising ground in a bend of the River Foyle, and Columba could see the sea from it. Every tree in the great forest of oaks which it protects was dear to Columba – so much that his church could not be built with its chancel toward the east because that would have necessitated cutting down some of his beloved oaks. There is a poem attributed to Columba –

> "Though I am affrighted truly
> By death and by Hell
> I am more affrighted
> By the sound of an axe in Derry."

There is an interesting legend about Columba's residence in Derry. There came a spendthrift and a poor man to him seeking alms. He gave a penny to the poor man and a coin worth much more to the spendthrift. Those who were with him thought it strange that Columba would give more to the spendthrift than to the poor man. Columba sensed this and told some of his monks to follow the two recipients of his gifts. The monks followed the two men to town and there found the spendthrift spending his money and freely sharing it with every needy person. The poor man they found dead with the penny sewn up with a large store of money in his clothing - for he had been a miser. They came back with these tidings to Columba.

Then the saint said: "You wondered that I gave more to the spendthrift than to the poor man. But God told me that the poor man would not live long, and however long he lived he would not put the money to good use for himself or for anyone else, but would hide it as he had already hidden his treasure. God told me, too, that though the spendthrift would not keep his money long, yet he would be generous with it and give freely to others."

Stories like this were obviously made after Columba's passing, since there was no coinage in the Ireland of his time. However, the story illustrates the Saint's reputation for humor, or for ironic ways of teaching his lessons. Another story tells of the Saint meeting a stupid dull-witted fellow and wishing him a clever and handsome wife. To a fine, proud youth he wished a stupid and lazy wife. Only by such marriages as these, he told his brethren, could things be evened in this world.

In spite of his constant journeying, Columba continued to keep in touch with all his foundations. He became a well-known figure all over Ireland as well as in the islands round her coast. Although the kings and chiefs were always at war among themselves, they all respected the monks, who were allowed to travel about unmolested. A portion of the plunder from their wars was given to the monasteries, a custom that may have come about from the belief the gifts might atone for the robbery and killing they had committed.

Columba had a great love of the sea. He later wrote of his delight in rowing his coracle (boat) round the shore of Derry and his love of "the roar of and thunder of the waves." Many years later when living on Iona, Columba expressed his love for Derry in a poem:

> "Were all the tribute of Scotia mine
> From its midland to its borders,
> I would give all for one little cell
> In my beautiful Derry."

For the next fifteen years Columba traveled over the length and breadth of Ireland, teaching, preaching and founding churches and monasteries. He is believed to have established thirty-seven monasteries including the famous monastery of Durrow (Dairmagh). His method was to find a suitable site, usually in an inhabited area where a church was needed, then go boldly to the owner to ask for it. When permission was given, he erected the requisite buildings - working with his own hands when necessary and installing carefully trained workers before moving on.

The monastery of Kells (in West Mead) was specially loved by Columba who prophesied that it should become the "loftiest cloister" on earth. This prophecy was fulfilled for after Columba's death, when his monks were driven from Iona by Scandinavian pirates, Kells became the headquarters of the Columban monks who founded there "a new city of Columcille." Kells is most generally known for its illuminated copy of the Gospels, which is usually ascribed to Columba but most probably dates from the eighth century.

Columba has been described as a "Celt of the Celts" with all the characteristics of that race; proud, arrogant, excitable temperament and yet with a lively sense of justice and honesty. Yet there was another side to Columba's character; a lover of beauty, a poet to whom poetry came as naturally as speech to the ordinary man, a scholar and a servant of God. In a strangely mixed character Columba united a reputation for sanctity with that quality of unscrupulous craft that earned him the nickname, "Crimthann," (fox).

Columba could never forget that he was also a prince of the royal-blood of Ireland - "a king's son of reddened valour" as St. Cormac is said to have styled him on one occasion. (Adamnan by Rrves 1857 -p. 269).

Along with his evangelical activities, Columba was keenly interested and closely implicated in all the political movements of his time to the end of advancing the cause of his Scotic countrymen. Some of Columba's missionary ventures into the land of the Picts seem to have been more political than religious, a point overlooked by most historians.

The turning point in Columba's life came when he was forty years of age. He was at the height of his fame, known throughout Ireland as a great saint and churchman, a mighty organizer of monasteries, "multarum columna ecclesiarum." (Adamnan, Bk 111, Ch. XXII pg. 184). In the ancient "Feilire of Angus" we find a description of what he looked like at this time; "His skin was white, his face broad and fair and radiant, lit up with large grey luminous eyes; his long and well-shaped head was crowned, except where he wore his frontal tonsure, with close and curling hair. His voice was clear and resonant, yet sweet with more than the sweetness of the bards."

Columba was an eager student of the Scriptures, in days when there were no printed books and when manuscripts were rare and difficult of access. He used to go about the country seeking for manuscripts to copy, the only way in those days to secure a book for oneself. There was no limit to what a man with a scholar's mind and temperament would go, to obtain for his own, a copy of the Gospels. So when his beloved teacher returned from a trip to Rome, bringing with him "beautiful copies of the sacred books", it was natural that Columba should be eager to see them. It was practically certain that there was among them a copy of the Vulgate (St. Jerome's new translation of the Gospels) which was by that time being used in Rome, but had never before reached Ireland.

Finian was hesitant of lending his precious manuscript but the eager anxiety of his student to see the new version of the Gospels, something nearer the very words his Master had spoken than the old version with which up till then he had had to be content, touched his spirit. Columba was allowed the privilege to have access to the manuscript where it was kept in the monastery chapel. But no sooner had Columba begun to study it than he knew he must have a copy for himself, so he could study and meditate on it at leisure.

Without asking Finian's permission which he knew would be refused, Columba contrived to stay behind the others in church, and began there to secretly copy the manuscript. Legend has that the illumination of the church by candle light led to the discovery of the copying. Finian was angry and demanded all copies be surrendered to him. Columba refused to give up his transcripts and the High King of Ireland, Diarmait MacCerball and a distant relative of Columba was called upon to settle the dispute.

According to the accounts, the case was heard at Tara when the national assembly (Triennial Feis) was being held. Abbot Finian spoke first, "I come, High King" he said in effect, "to demand justice against Columcille. He copied my Gospels of Holy Jerome's text without my knowledge and refuses to give me the copy. I say that as the original is mine, the copy is mine too."

We can picture the tall, austere, grey-eyed Columba answering with vehemence. "And I say, Diarmait, that Finian's book has lost nothing by my copying from it, and that it would not be right that the holy things in that book should be hid or kept by one person to himself; nor yet that any person should be held from writing or reading them, or spreading them among the people. I say that it was lawful for me to copy the Gospel, if I and the people gained thereby, without hurt to Finian or his book."

The king, having no case-law of copyright to guide his judgment gave a decision which has passed into proverb. He cited a legal adage, "le gach a buinin"; "To every cow belongs her calf, and to every book its son-book." Needless to say, Columba was angered by what he considered an unjust decision. The breach between him and the High-King was widened by a second incident which happened during the games at Tara's festival.

During the game of hurling the spears, the son of King of Connacht unintentionally killed one of Diarmait's servants. The lad fled to Columba for sanctuary since death was the punishment for breaking the peace of Tara. The indignant king sent officers to arrest the fugitive. Columba denied them approach to his dwelling on the royal hill, but they broke down the churchmen's resistance and seized the unhappy youth.

This affront to Columba following the humiliating judgment against him by Diarmait awoke all the passionate vindictiveness in Columba's soul. He indiscreetly made open threats against the king. He would go to his kinsmen (northern Clan Niall) and organize a rebellion against the southern Clan Niall and their king Diarmait. The king being told of these threats decided to send riders to follow and seize Columba before he could reach Ulster.

Columba had traveled as far as Monasterboice and was lodged with Buite's monks when word reached him of the king's plans. The northward road was watched by the king's men who planned on capturing him as he passed. The next morning Columba sent his companions northward by the accustomed road, but he took a solitary way over the descending moor, composing, the old books say, a poetic prayer of protection as he went:

> "M'aenaran dam isa sliabh
> A Ri grian rob soraid set -
> Nim nesa ec inc mend
> Andas no bend trichait chet . . ."

What purports to be Columba's poem is recorded in the Book of Leister, written in the twelfth century and also found in other Irish manuscripts. The lines, though ancient, are not ancient enough in language to be authentically his, but probably based on some other composition which was really composed by Columba. The imagery is characteristically that used by Columba. The following translation of the entire poem is made by Dr. James Carney: (Eigse, II, 2)

A lonely man I go upon the mountain moor: O King of Suns, let the way be safe. Death in its snares is not nearer to me than if I walked with thirty thousand to guard me.

With thirty thousand around me, of young, strong-bodied helpers, yet if harsh death were decreed, no strength could avert it.

There is no safeguard for the son of man if he be doomed; yet none has heard of a pathway which the undoomed might not pass in safety.

Though some may desire my death, or covet my belongings, yet till the fair Lord wills it, that which he meditates he cannot compass.

No mere man can compass my life to-day; nore day take it save the King who made the summer day, the Sovereign of heaven and of earth.

Nothing can turn me from my journey, I fear no omen; the sod whereon my burial stone shall be raised, towards that I must travel.

Naught can turn me from my lonely way: the mortal world shapeth me, but cannot send me forth; I leave not life till my doom is decreed - the nut falls not till He plucks it.

The hero who ventures his fair body against fierce warriors at the ford, though reckless, he is not nearer to death than the cautious one who stands in the rear.

Though the traveller rightly seeks protection on his journey, in whatsoever safeguard he goes, what is his safeguard against death?

Howsoever often a man may avoid death, the day of peril comes upon him at the appointed end of life.

I put myself under the protection of the high and glorious God, Father of the nine ranks of holy angels; may He not let me fall into the horrors of stark death, or into fear, though I go lonely on the mountain moor.

At length Columba came safely into Ulster and had no trouble persuading the kinsmen to take up arms against the clan of the High-King. They were already discontented of their own suzerain - they claimed the High-Kingship belonged by right to them. The decision against their kinsman, Columba, and a member of their own ruling house, was considered an insult against their clan. Believing their honor to be at stake, they rushed impetuously to arms.

In the meanwhile, Diarmait was leading his forces north to assert his authority against the malcontents. The two forces met at Cooldrevny (A.D. 561) in fierce combat. Columba's clan was successful and Diarmait had to flee for his life leaving his army decimated. The losses for both sides totaled some three thousand men. Both sides resolutely condemned the other for the great loss of Irish blood for a worldly cause. Columba, however, was saddened by the carnage on the battlefield, and accepted responsibility. When offered the throne after the battle he is reported to have said: -

"It may not be. Long ago, I gave up my claim to the Kingdom of Ireland, that I might seek the Kingdom of God. Ill have I served the heavenly kingdom, and ill have I served Ireland in that I have caused the men of Ireland to shed one another's blood. Men lie dead through the pride of a man of peace, I will not rest," the saddened abbot went on, "till

I have won for God the souls of as many as have fallen in this battle. And as for Diarmait, MacCearvaill, let him be High-King still, and let the men of Eire seek henceforward to live together in peace."

The legend may be exaggerated, but the main facts of the story are true. Columba was blamed for the battle. At the Synod of Teltown, in Meath, Columba's conduct over the copied manuscript was censured. He himself was ex-communicated. Later, on the intercession of St. Brendan of Birr, the sentence was withdrawn. Some historians say, Columba was banished from Ireland, while others report, he, filled with remorse of the great loss of life, voluntarily exiled himself from his native land.

Colmcille's House

Another story is that Columba, feeling public opinion was against him, took the advice of his "soul friend" St. Molaise of Devenish in Lough Erne. Molaise advised him to disappear and hinted that he might ease his burdened conscience by winning in foreign lands as many souls for Christ as the lives thrown away in the frivolous quarrel that culminated in the slaughter of Cooldrevny. In any event, it was a penitent Columba that sailed away from Ireland, in A.D. 563 with twelve companions, four of them kinsmen.

The little party crossed the Irish Channel in coracles of wicker and hide. The coracle boats of that period were frail crafts with a framework of slender, pliable branches covered by hides made taunt by leather thongs laced to the top edge of the frame. After an initial soaking the hides were allowed to dry in the sun, molding themselves to the contour of the boat. Such a boat made a reasonable buoyant sea-going craft which would hold up to the battering of the rough Hebridean seas.

An old print depicting the embarking of St. Columba and his followers from the shores of Erin, for his missionary work in Scotland

What Columba's thoughts were as he saw the green hills of Erin sink below the horizon, we gather from the lines he wrote on the voyage:

> "How swift is the speed of my coracle
> Its stern turned to Derry;
> I grieve at my errand o'er the noble sea
> Travelling to Alba of the ravens.
> My foot in my good little coracle
> My sad heart is still bleeding:
> Weak is the man who cannot lead;
> Totally blind are all the ignorant,
> A grey eye looks back to Erin,
> A grey eye full of tears,
> It shall never see again
> The men of Erin nor their wives.
> While I stand on the deck of my barque
> I stretched my vision o'er the briny sea
> Westwards to Erin."

Columba and his companions first landed in Argyll, where he visited his kinsmen in Scottish Dalriada, before sailing on to Oronsay, a little island which is separated only at flood-tide from Colonsay, beyond Islay. Here on Oronsay, the little group of voyagers stayed for some time. On one very clear day, Columba climbed a low hill and gazed southward past Islay - and saw the dim shore of Ireland some sixty miles away. He could no longer stay, having pledged to himself to go out of sight of his native country.

Again Columba put to sea sailing northward. After sailing about twenty miles they sighted the land that was to become their new home.

IONA

"Lone Isle, though storms have round thy turrets rode,

Thou wert the Temple of the living God,

And taught earth's millions at His shrine to bow,

Though desolation wraps thy glories now,

Still thou wilt be a marvel through all time

For what they hast been; and the dead who rest

Around the fragments of thy walls sublime,

Once taught the world and harbour'd many a guest,

And rules the warriors of each northern clime,

Thou'rt in the world like some benighted one,

Home of the mighty that have passed away:

Hail! sainted Isle" thou are a holy spot

Engraved on many hearts; and thou art worth

A pilgrimage, for glories long gone by,

Thou nobliest College of all the ancient earth,

Virtue and Truth, Religion itself shall die

Ere thou canst perish from the chart of fame,

Or darkness shroud the halo of thy name."

                                                           D.Moore

THE ARRIVAL OF COLUMBA

It was on the 12th day of May 563, the eve of Whitsunday (fiftieth day after Easter, or Pentecost) that Columba and his companions rounded the south end of the Isle of Mull in the Inner Hebridean seas. Ahead of them were the dreaded Torren Rocks, the Merry Men of Robert Lewis Stevenson. Passing through the labyrinth of rocks they made their way into a small bay, which to this day retains the name "Port of the Coracle" (Port-na-Churaich), although it is better known as "Columba's Bay."

Columba's Bay

The bay is flanked with high rocks and is divided in two by a low rock islet, which forms a kind of natural pier when the weather and tide are favorable. The beach is covered with colored pebbles of great variety and beauty and as the tide is receding they sparkle like gem stones. Out in the bay is a reef of translucent green serpentine from which tiny fragments are broken off and cast ashore by the waves. These pebbles, which have become scarce, are known as "Iona Stone" or "St. Columba's Stone". The local inhabitants consider them to be a charm against drowning.

Tradition tells us that the monks drew their coracle up over the terrace of stones to the grassy slope at the top of the bay, and there dug a deep grave in which they buried it that they might not be tempted to return to Ireland. A grassy mound supposedly over the burial site was excavated and no remains of a coracle was found. It is now believed to have been an ancient grave mound of the Stone Age. Other mounds and green humps nearby my be signs of former dwellings.

Rock Caverns

   At the western end of the beach are a number of curious rock cairns whose origin and purpose is lost in antiquity. It was once thought they might have been the burial places of islanders who anciently lived on the island several centuries before Columba. Excavations of some of the cairns found only stones.

   After their coracle was buried, Columba climbed the nearest hill to be sure Ireland could not be seen from the neighboring heights, the southern horizon showing only a line of sea. Here he would remain and found his Christian colony. The little hill has ever since been marked with a cairn which is known as the "Caurn-cul-ri-Erin" or "Cairn with the back turned upon Erin." Before finally deciding, however, the party would inspect the island.

Cairn with the back turned upon Erin

Seeing a cone-shaped hill toward the north, they cautiously made their way toward it. The first mile was over rocks and untellable ground. But further north the lush pastoral ground of Iona was encountered, which must have given them encouragement. At the foot of the hill they had seen, today known as Dun-I, they found shelter from the gales which swept across the Atlantic and nearby a small stream of water, the only considerable stream on the island.

On the south side of Dun-I Columba saw a little isolated hollow. There, later he was to erect some small huts for prayers and meditation. Built of successive layers of flat stones projecting inward, finally meeting at the top, they have the appearance of an inverted bowl. They are commonly known as "bee-hive huts." One small hut apart from the others may have been the one used by Columba.

Although Iona is a rocky island with rocks protruding at frequent intervals through the grassy turf, there are heather covered hills sloping into tracts of thyme and wild clover covering shelly sand which are suitable for the support of flocks and herds. The remainder adapted for the growth of corn.

Druid Temple

On the east side of the island in a sheltered corner that lay between the hill and the Sound, Columba found the standing stones of a Druid Temple. There he decided to build his settlement and his church. The site is believed to be about 200 yards north of the present Cathedral of Iona. In a sense, Iona was a sacred place before Columba. Many writers tell of Iona being sacred to the Druids and a burial place of their priests and kings. It was known as "Innis nan Druinidh" (Island of the Druids). Perhaps this may have influenced Columba in deciding to stay there and make it a truly holy place.

In pre-Christian days, the religion of the Celtic people, whose ancient territory, of which Ireland and Scotland formed a part, was Druidism. Through his investigations, made over 200 years ago, the English antiquarian, William Stukely, asserts that true Druidism was introduced into Britain from the Bible lands about the period of Abraham. He further states that it was undoubtedly derived from the original, undefiled religion of the patriarchs.

Thus, Druidism is older than the Celtic Druidic priesthood that came into existence just a few centuries before the Roman conquest of Britain. While no literary documents exist to prove the date of the establishment of Druidism in Britain, the educational system adopted by the Druids is traced to about 1800 B.C. when Hu Gadarn Hyscion (Isaacson?) or "Hu the Mighty," led a party of settlers from Asia Minor to Britain. A descendant of Abraham, Hu the Mighty's coming to Britain provides one of the first recorded instances of the fulfillment of prophecy (Gen. 28:14) that the "seed" of Abraham would spread abroad, to the four points of the compass.

Iona was situated exactly halfway between the Christian Scots of Argyll and the pagan Picks. Thus it was admirably suited for Columba's purposes. The migration of the Argyll settlers from Dalriada, in northern Ireland, started during the early years of the Christian era. At that time the tribes of Erin were engaged in bitter fighting among themselves and the sight of the distant shores of Alba, Scotland, must have been seen as a place of refuge for the strife weary Scots. Known in the Latin of the period as "Scotti," they are reputed to have made their first crossing in the second century A.D., establishing contact with the native tribes who inhabited the region of Argyll at that time.

Following these earlier smaller infiltrations in Argyll, history records that in 489 A.D. a larger expedition arrived. This was led by Fergus, Angus and Loarn, the three sons of Erc, King of Dunseverick in Antrim. They brought with them a fleet of ships and one hundred fifty men, and soon divided the land of Argyll among them. Fergus, the eldest, made his headquarters at Dunaad, once a hilltop fort of the Picts, near Locgilphead. Angus settled in Islay and Loarn chose the area centered around Dunollie and Oban, which still bears his name. They called their new homeland Dalriada, after their place of origin in Ireland.

Existing records are hazy as to the exact relationship of the Dalriadans with the native Pictish tribes, of which we know very little. The relationship could not have been particularly friendly according to a report of a battle (in A.D. 560) between the two groups in which the Dalriandan leader was killed and the Pictish King Brude regained control of the area from his capital in Inverness. This was a bleak period in the early history of the Scots and their future prospects in Pickland seemed very much in doubt until, with the arrival of their fellow-countryman Columba, there came a dramatic change in their fortunes.

There is a story that a small "anomalous" church existed on the island before the arrival of Columba to service the burial grounds of the Dalriada Scots. According to the old Irish "Life" quoted by Dr. Skene, "Two bishops who were on the island came to lead him by the hand out of it (Columba's coracle) but God now revealed to Columcille that they were not true bishops, whereby they left the island to him when he told them of their history." (Celtic Scotland, vol. II, pp. 24, 34, 49, 88) Columba apparently refused to recognize them as real bishops and so they left the island to him.

Imaginative sketch of the Columban Monastery (looking east: Columba's cell in foreground)

THE IONA COMMUNITY

There were twelve men with Columba at first. Soon their friends from Ireland followed including Britons and Saxons, and Iona was humming with activity. The first order of work was the preparation of the ground for farming. Corn was planted while a small church was erected surrounded by small bee-hive huts of wood or wattle for the monks. Somewhat apart from the others stood the Abbot's house on rising ground. Other buildings were a "hospitium" or guest house, a cook-house and a refectory for common meals built around a flat glacial-carried boulder which has now disappeared.

The whole establishment was enclosed by a fencible dry-built stone wall and an earthen bank. Outside the earthwork was another cluster of buildings consisting of a cow-shed, two barns, (one next to the settlement and the other near the fields), a stable, a carpenter's shop, a mill, and a kiln. The foundation of the kiln can be clearly seen today, it having been built of stone because the fire used to dry the corn could easily have set fire to a building built of wood and wattle. The position of the mill is also certain for it stood beside the only stream on Iona capable of turning a mill-wheel.

Our knowledge of Columba's community comes from the writings of Adamnan, the Abbot of Iona from A.D. 679 until his death in 704. Adamnan was born only twenty-seven years after Columba's death in A.D. 597. He belonged to the same tribe as Columba and came to Iona as a young man where he lived with many brethren trained by Columba himself. When Adamnan was fifty-five, Columba's mantle fell upon him. Adamnan's book the "Life of St. Columba" was written about one hundred years after the death of Columba.

Because Adamnan thought in Gaelic and wrote in Latin, some scholars state that his style of writing is difficult to understand. However, his "biography of Columba is considered the most complete piece of biography that all Europe can boast of, not only as so early a period but throughout the Middle Ages." (Pinkerton) It is also the only record of the church in Scotland at that time and makes Columba known to us in a way which no other historical character of that date is known. The description of Columba's last days had been acknowledged as "one of the tide-marks of medieval prose . . . one of the most exquisite pieces of pure biography ever written . . . a very gem of literature."

Adamnan described Columba's church as constructed of fine timbers brought to Iona from the nearby Isle of Mull. It had one large enclosure with an altar upon which the holy vessels were laid. A side chapel served as a sacristy and contained the monastery bell. The bell was an important part of the monastic life. One of the chief duties of the smith attached to any monastery was to make bells for all the members. They were small and simple consisting of a sheet of metal having the edges bent over and riveted together. A loop of iron was let in the top and the whole dipped in molten bronze which ran into and filled up the joints.

By the time the buildings were finished, the membership of the monastic community had grown to about 150 souls. They consisted of workers from Ireland and Saxons from Britain drawn to Iona by the fame of Columba. An old Irish verse reads:

> "Wondrous the warriors who abode in Hi
> Thrice fifty in the monastic rule
> With their boats along the main sea
> Three score men a-rowing."

When new penitents arrived on Iona they were required to confess their sins on their knees before the whole community. They were then given a penance "according to the judgment of the Saint." Sometimes it would be exile for a number of years to some outlying island. Exile was the heaviest punishment Columba could conceive, perhaps feeling his self-banishment so acutely.

These Iona monks were not hermits or recluses, characteristic in later years. They were active men who lived a community life, supporting themselves by their own toil and whose whole aim in life was to spread the good news of Jesus Christ. Each member of the "Family" as they became known, took a vow that he willingly forsook the world and joined the community to "win souls for Christ." Each member was then tonsured (the whole front part of their head being shaved from ear to ear) according to the Irish custom which had prevailed since the time of St. Patrick.

Their first job in importance was attendance at the services held everyday in the little church. It is believed that there were six services every day, with more on "solemn days," but we read that the monks who engaged in farm-work did not have to attend all the services. They all studied languages (Latin, Greek and Gaelic); they read the Scriptures and especially learned the Psalms by heart.

The family of Iona was divided into three classes: the "senoirs" who worked chiefly at making copies of the Gospels and the Psalms; the "working brethren" who were the most numerous; and the physically robust who did all the strenuous work of the community. They made the food, herded the sheep and cattle and worked the farms. They also built the boats and sailed the seas on errands of necessity and mercy. The third class was the "juniors". Some of them came from long distances to live the arduous life of the community as a voluntary penance.

BITH IND UATHAD ILLUEE FO LEITH

"Be alone in a separate place near a chief city, if thy conscience is not prepared to be in common with the crowd.

Be always naked or much thou possessest of anything whether of clothing, or food, or drink, let it be at the command of the senior and at his disposal, for it is not befitting a religious to have any distinction of property with his own free brother.

Let a fast place, with one door, enclose thee.

A few religious men to converse with thee of God and His Testament; to visit thee on days of solemnity; to strengthen thee in the testaments of God and the narratives of the Scriptures.

A person too who would talk with thee in idle words, or of the world; or who murmurs at what he cannot remedy or prevent, but who would distress thee more should he be a tattler between friends and foes, thou shalt not admit him to thee, but at once give him thy benediction should he deserve it.

Let thy servant be a discreet, religious, not tale-telling man, who is to attend continually on thee, with moderate labour, but always ready.

Yield submission to every rule that is of devotion.

A mind prepared for red martyrdom.

A mind fortified and steadfast for white martyrdom..

Forgiveness from the heart to every one.

Constant prayers for those who trouble thee.

Fervour in singing the office for the dead, as if every faithful dead was a particular friend of thine.

Hymns for souls to be sung standing.

Let thy vigils be constant from eve to eve, under the direction of another person.

Three labours in the day, viz, prayers, work, and reading.

The work to be divided into three parts, viz, thine own work, and the work of thy place, as regards its real wants; secondly, thy share of the brethren's work; lastly, to help the neighbor's, viz., by instruction, or writing, or sewing garments, or whatever labour they may be in want of, *ut Dominus ait, "Non apparebis ante me vacuus."*

Everything in its proper order: Nemo enim coronabitur nisi qui legitime certaverit.

The food at the community was very simple, consisting chiefly of porridge, bread, milk, eggs and fish. Occasionally a seal was killed and its flesh was eaten and sometimes a salmon was caught off Mull. Adamnan mentions the monastery had a cook, a baker, a griddle for roasting beef and mutton. While porridge was the chief food, meal and flour was also baked into loaves, generally mixed with water. Sometimes milk or honey was added and as a great luxury the roe of a salmon was added to the bread. The loaves were baked on a flat stone supported over a fire fueled by peat from a moss bed near the south side of the island.

Corn grown on the island was ground into coarse and fine flour and stored in wooden chests. The grinding was done at first with a hand-quern, such as still used in remote parts of the Western Highland, examples of which have been dug up on Iona. Later the grinding was done by a water-mill, the wheel of which was turned by the stream that flowed past the barn and the smithy. When the number of monks on Iona increased and there was not enough grain on the island to support them, Columba established a home-farm on the nearby low-lying land of Tiree, to provide the mother-island with food. According to Adamnan the settlement on Tiree was in the charge of Columba's cousin, Baithene.

Milk was provided from cows seemingly to have been grazed some distance from the monastery, for we read of some monks bringing him milk in leather bags and wooden pitchers. Sometimes the milk was driven home in a little cart drawn by Columba's well-known white horse. Columba was regarded as the patron saint of cattle, and the shepherd driving his herd out to pasture was accompanied by Columba's "herding blessing." Sheep were raised for meat and material for their clothes. They used parchment made of sheepskin for manuscripts.

The monks wore coarse habits of tough undyed wool over a tunic of finer material. On feast days they wore white. Columba wore a cowl (cuculla) but whether his monks wore this is not stated by Adamnan. In bad weather an outer cloak was allowed. The sandals of the monks were of hide laced together by leather thongs. These were removed on sitting down to meals. The hours of meals differed with the seasons of the year. Wednesday and Friday were the regular fast days, but the rule was relaxed between Easter and Pentecost. During Lent the fast was kept till the evening of every day except Sunday, when milk, bread and eggs were allowed during the day. On Sundays and feast days or when guests were present the food was more ample and included some delicacies.

At night the monks slept on pallets of heather or bracken with a blanket on top. They lay down in their habits as they rose periodically during the night for devotions. Their pillows were generally of wool, though Columba's own pillow was of stone and is still to be seen in the sanctuary of the present Abbey of Iona. This stone was found near the place where Columba was first buried. The stone is about twenty inches long and had a cross incised on it. Columba's bed is also said to have been less comfortable than that of his monks. Tradition mentions a stone "flag" with a hide laid over the stone.

The role of the monastic community of Iona, as in Ireland, enforced strict observance of religious duty and ascetic practice. Obedience, celibacy, poverty, caution, reason in speech and humility - these were its main features. The monks called their leader "Father" and to him they were children, to one another, "brethren". From the earliest times the community is spoken of as the family of Hy. Up to that time, the island had been known in Gaelic as "Hy" or "Y", pronounced as "E" in English. After Columba settled there it soon became known throughout the highlands as the "Island-of-Columba-of-the-Church." In Gaelic, it was known as "I-Choluim-Chille." However by whatever name it was known, Iona was always associated with the things of the Spirit.

Columba called his followers, the "Soldiers of Christ" (Milites Christi). He himself being known as the "Warrior of the Island." These names were not merely figures of speech, for in those warlike days the monks often had to defend themselves as well as those who claimed their protection. They carried arms as a matter of course as late as the days of Adamnan (A.D. 679 to 848).

The monks lived strenuous lives doing the work on the farms, carrying grain home from the fields and flour from the mill to the kitchen in between their devotions. When each day's work was done, Columba rendered his monks the ancient service of washing their feet, following in all things the example of Christ. Columba was always concerned with their well-being, whether they were with him on Iona tempted by evil spirits, or jealousy, depression, or whether they were in danger at sea while doing errands at his request.

Near Iona was the little rocky island of Soas where seals or sea-calves bred. Soas was regarded as the community's private seal farm and intruders were told that the seals there were "ours by right." However when strangers were caught stealing seals, Columba offered to gladly give them sheep in place of the seals they had in their possession. The seals provide the community with skins for covering in winter and seal-oil for burning in their "crusties." For artificial light in the long winter nights they may have used candles, for these were known to have been used in Ireland and Britain as early as the time of St. Patrick. (A.D. 389-461). Fires were started by flint and tinder.

Much of the early traffic about Scotland went by water. Coastwise sailing was often easier than overland routes. In the fiords and islands of Dalriada, efficient boats were a first necessity. In the days of the Celtic saints, there seem to have been three sorts of boats used: plank-built boats like our present-day designs, dug-outs made by hollowing out a large tree trunk, and skin-covered boats or coracles. Adamnan speaks of "long boats of hewn pine and oak." In the same account he also records coracles towing oak logs from the Loch Shiel district back to Iona to repair the monastery.

Coracles or curraghs are made of skins stretched over a frame-work of rods. They are light and ride well over the crests of the waves. They are both rowed and sailed. Adamnan gives several accounts of the Iona boats weathering bad storms. One story tells of a boat caught in the Corryvreckan whirlpools between the islands of Jura and Scarba and coming successfully through the ordeal. Small coracles were carried to make crossings of inland lakes.

Columba spent thirty-four years on Iona. Perhaps one of the reasons why Columba chose Iona was that he wanted to create a new pattern of life and knew such an island was suitable. It was large enough with a plentiful supply of fresh water and soil sufficiently fertile to support a community. Its small size and its windswept exposed west side would not attract attention by Irish settlers or Picts. Its serenity and beauty was conducive to the religious life Columba wanted to instill in his followers.

Columba's days were spent in teaching men new ways of working with ploughs and sickles, seeding and harvesting, and growing food and eating it. He taught his monks a new culture; the use of pen and ink and the new business of writings words on parchments. In our world today it is hard to imagine how difficult life must have been on Iona. The difficulties consisted of getting material and training men to make things. It was work, year after year after year; the constantly demanding work of industry and teaching men to be farmers, fishermen, carpenters and metal workers.

A PAGE OF THE CATHACH

The name Cathach (pronounced *Caah*) means "Battler." It is thus explained in O'Donnell's *Life of Columcille* (1532), in the account of Cooldrevny (§ 178, ed. A. O'Kelleher and G. Schoepperle, p. 183). The *Cathach* for a sooth is the name of that book by reason whereof the battle was fought.

The Cathach is now preserved in the Library of the Royal Irish Academy, within a beautiful silver and gold *cumdach* or shrine, which (as we learn from an inscription on its base) was made to enclose the greatly venerated book at the order of Domnall MacRobartaigh, *Coarb* of Kells *(circa 1062-1098)*.

THE IONA SCRIBES

The copying of the Scriptures was one of the chief occupations of the Iona Community monks. There was a separate hut where those engaged in copying could work and where the manuscripts were kept. Writing in Columba's day was an art. The pens were of goose, crow or swan quills, cut by the monks who also prepared their own ink. The writings was done sometimes on wax tablets (with styles) but for the Gospels, parchment was used. The scribes were so awed by the wonder of the Gospel message that they felt compelled to make their copies as worthy as they could of the Truth the Scriptures contained. Only the finest work was worthy to be used to spread the Good News of Jesus Christ.

Columba devoted a lot of time to the copying of texts, particularly liturgical texts. So important was this task that Adamnan placed it alongside praying and reading, when writing of Columba's devotion to duty. Columba's love of manuscripts is undoubtedly known, for he was greatly upset if one was damaged from getting wet or had ink split over it. It was also a problem if the scribe made a mistake while copying it, because corrections were liable to spoil the page.

It should be remembered that each book in Iona's considerable library had been copied by hand requiring an enormous amount of painstaking time to produce, as was the case in all libraries until the invention of the printing press in the fifteenth century. Columba insisted that each of his monks give themselves wholeheartedly to the job at hand, whether it be copying, praying, teaching or any of the other tasks of the monastery. That he gave himself wholeheartedly to what he was doing is illustrated by an amusing story which had a definite ring of authenticity.

"Once, one of the brethren, Molua Ua Briuin by name came to the Saint while he was engaged in copying a manuscript and asked him, 'Please bless this implement which I have in my hand.' St. Columba did not look up, but continued to keep his eye on the book from which he was copying. However he reached his hand out a little way and, still holding his pen, made the sign of the cross. Molus took away the implement he had blessed, and later St. Columba asked Diarmait, his loyal servant, 'What was the implement I blessed for our brother?' 'A knife,' said

Diarmait, 'for the slaughtering of bulls or cattle.' 'I trust in my Lord,' added St. Columba, that the implement I have blessed will not harm man or beast.' According to the story, Molua found that the knife was useless for killing a bullock so the monks melted it down and used it to cast the iron tools of the monastery."

We know that Columba made many copies of the Gospels and the Psalter, called the "Cathach". The "Annals of Clonmacnoice" states that he wrote three hundred books with his own hand. It further states "they were all New Testaments and that he left a book with each of his churches." These copies were supposed, like everything belonging to Columba to possess supernatural powers. The monks believed that everything was possible to him. Although the stories of his "miracles" sound strange to our modern ears, they do show implicit trust and love his monks had for him. So powerful was his personality and close his sympathy with the monks and his friends, that they actually felt his prayers speeding to them when they were in trouble or danger. And who can say with certainty that God does not answer the prayers of a righteous man?

Hymn-singing was a regular part of the worship in Iona, and Adamnan writes of a book of the week's hymns written out by Columba with his own hand. This establishes that Columba wrote hymns for the use of the community. Tradition has it that he produced hundreds of these hymns. Of many of the hymns ascribed to Columba, we find a central theme and that is, praise of God precedes any petition. An expansive recitation of God's attributes came before a request for personal salvation. The following hymn is attributed to Columba.

> O helper of workers,
> Ruler of all the good,
> Guard on the ramparts
> And defender of the faithful,
> Who lift up the lowly
> And crush the proud,
> Ruler of the faithful,
> Enemy of the impenitent,
> Judge of all judges,
> Who punish those who err,
> Pure life of the living,

> Denying to none of the hopeful
> Your strength and help,
> I beg that me a little man
> Trembling and most wretched,
> Rowing through the infinite storm
> Of this age.
> Christ may draw after Him to the lofty
> Most beautiful haven of life
> . . . and unending
> Holy hymn forever,
> From the envy of enemies you lead me
> Into the joy of paradise.

Columba is said to have composed 150 poems, some in Latin and some in Gaelic. Only three manuscripts in his own handwriting exist today. Nearly eighty Gaelic poems exist which are ascribed to the Saint, but the language and the metrics prove them to belong, in their present form, to what is called Middle Irish period - the ninth to the twelfth centuries. The style and spirit of these pieces all agree with the known works of the Abbot and could be copies of older pieces, authentically his work.

Perhaps the most famous of the three compositions ascribed to Columba is his poem, the "Altus Prosator" written as a tribute to St. Gregory the Great. It is a majestic hymn of twenty-three verses, which begin with the successive letter of the Latin alphabet. The language is described as rugged, difficult, sometimes obscure. Besides the alphabetic form, which is Hebraic, there are Hebrew expressions and Hellenisms, indicating Columba's known acquaintance with the older ancient tongues. There are Holy Scriptures quoted, and the language indicates that the poet is familiar with the pre-Vulgate Text. The first verse of the Altus Prosator is as follows:

> Altus Prosator vetustus dierum et ingenitus
> Erat absque origine primordii et crepidine,
> Est et erit in saeoula saeoulorum infinita,
> Cut est uniqenitus Christus et Sanctus Spritus,
> Coaeternus in gloria Deitatis perpetuae
> Non tres deos depromimus sed unum Deum dicimus,
> Salva fide in personis tribus gloriosissimis.

Translation:
Abba, Father, high and might,
All days old and unbegotten,
Hath been without spring primordial,
Without base or limitation,
Is, and shall be, through the ages,
Never-ending, countless ages:
Christ, His Son, the Sole-begotten,
And the Holy Spirit likewise,
Co-eternal are in glory
Of the Everlasting Godhead.
Not three Gods do we account Them,
But One Godhead we proclaim Thee,
Save the faith when we pronounce Them,
One God in Three glorious persons.

One of the most famous books associated with the Iona community and traditionally written by Columba is the Book of Kells, now resting in the Trinity College Library in Dublin, Ireland. However the copy now extant, probably dates from the second half of the eighth century. Its place of origin remains uncertain. The most prevalent theory is that it was originally started by the Iona monks and taken by them incomplete to Kells around A.D. 806 and completed there.

The Book of Kells contains the four Gospels in Latin text. Its script is accompanied by large lavishly painted illuminated pages with intricate shapes and patterns. Within the lines themselves are brilliant decorations. (Only two of its 680 pages are without color.) Sometimes the decorations in the script assume the proportion of major illuminations, as in the treatment of the Beatitudes, in St. Matthew's Gospel, where the whole length of the page is decorated with the eight capital Bs. Each B is formed out of serpent bodies, four with human heads, four with the heads of birds and all colored in turquoise, violet and golden brown. At other times the decorations are small, obscure, and often surprisingly comic representations of insects, animals, birds and human figures, peering out from behind letters, lurking in the corners of pages, floating between the lines or in the margins.

The Opening Pages of
St. Matthew, St. Mark and St. John

Throughout the whole of the Book of Kells one of the most striking features is the repeated emphasis on the four Evangelists through their symbols, the Man for Matthew, the Lion for Mark, the Calf for Luke and the Eagle for John. These symbols are depicted again and again together, but each time with a variation in presentation. In the first chapter of the prophet Ezekiel, a vision of four, winged, human figures is described, each with four faces, those of a man, a lion, an ox and an eagle.

BOOK OF KELLS
St. Luke XIII v. 6. Detail of initial letter: Di

celtic art

*The West Door
Iona Abbey*

THE DEATH OF ST. COLUMBA

The story of Columba's last days and death is best told by the picturesque minuteness of detail by Adamnan. The following is the translation of Bishop Forbes taken from Adamnan by Reeves, 1874 - pp. 94-98:

One day in the month of May the old man, worn out with age, went in a cart to visit some of the brethren who were at work. And having found them on the western side of the island, he began to speak to them, saying, "During the Paschal solemnities in the month of April now past, with desire have I desired to depart to Christ the Lord, as He had allowed me, if I preferred it. But lest a joyous festival should be turned for you into mourning, I thought it better to put off for a little longer the time of my departure from the world." The beloved monks all the while they were hearing this sad news were greatly afflicted, and he endeavored as well as he could too cheer them with words of consolation. Then having done this, he turned his face to the east, still seated as he was in his cart, and blessed the island with its inhabitants . . .

A few days afterwards, while he was celebrating the solemn offices of the Mass as usual on the Lord's Day, the face of the venerable man, as his eyes were raised to heaven, suddenly appeared as if suffused with a ruddy glow, for, as it is written, "a glad heart maketh a cheerful countenance." (Proverbs 15:13) For at that same hour he alone saw an Angel of the Lord hovering above within the walls of his oratory; and as the lovely and tranquil aspect of the holy Angels infuses joy and exultation into the hearts of the elect, this was the cause of that sudden joy infused into the blessed man. When those who were present on the occasion inquired as to the cause of that joy with which he was evidently inspired, the Saint looking upwards gave them this reply, "Wonderful and unspeakable is the subtlety of the angelic nature. For lo! An Angel of the Lord, who was sent to demand a certain deposit dear to God, hath, after looking down upon us within the church, and blessing us, returned again through the roof of the church, without leaving any trace of his passage out." Thus spoke the Saint. But none of the bystanders could understand what kind of a deposit the Angel was sent to demand. Our patron, however, gave the name of a holy deposit to his own soul that had been entrusted to him by God . . .

In the end of this same week, that is on the day of the Sabbath, (Saturday) the venerable man and his faithful attendant, Diarmait, went to bless the barn, which was near at hand. When the Saint had entered in and blessed it, and the two heaps of winnowed corn that were in it, he gave expression to his thanks in these words, saying: "I heartily congratulate my beloved monks, that this year also, if I am obliged to depart from you, you will have a sufficient supply for the year." On hearing this, Diarmait, his attendant, began to feel sad, and said "This year at this time, Father, thou very often vexest us, by so frequently making mention of thy leaving us." But the Saint replied to him, "I have a little secret address to make to thee, and if thou wilt promise me faithfully not to reveal it to anyone before my death, I shall be able to speak to thee with more freedom about my departure." When his attendant had on bended knees made the promise as the Saint desired, the venerable man thus resumed his address. "This day in the Holy Scriptures is called the Sabbath, which means rest. And this day is indeed a Sabbath for me, for it is the last day of my present laborious life, and on it I rest after the fatigues of my labours; and this night at midnight, which commenceth the solemn Lord's Day, I shall, according to the sayings of Scripture, go the way of our fathers. For already my Lord Jesus Christ deigneth to invite me; and to Him, I say, in the middle of the night shall I depart at His invitation. For so it hath been revealed to me by the Lord Himself." The attendant hearing these sad words began to weep bitterly, and the Saint endeavored to console him as well as he could.

After this the Saint left the barn, and in going back to the monastery rested half way, where a Cross, which was afterwards erected and is standing to this day, fixed into a mill-stone, may be observed on the roadside. While the Saint, as I have said, bowed down with old age, sat there to rest a little, behold there came up to him a white pack horse, the same that was used, as a willing servant, to carry the milk-vessels from the cow-shed to the monastery. It came up to the Saint, and, strange to say, laid its head on his bosom – inspired, I believe, by God to do so, as each animal is gifted with the knowledge of things according to the will of the Creator; and, knowing that its master was soon about to leave it, and that it would see him no more, began to utter plaintive cries, and like a human being to shed copious tears on the Saint's bosom, foaming and greatly wailing. The attendant seeing this, began to drive the weeping mourner away, but the Saint forbade him, saying, "Let it alone, as it is so fond of me – let it pour out its bitter-grief into my bosom. Lo! Thou, though thou art a man, and hast a rational soul, canst know nothing of my departure hence, except what I myself have just told thee: but to this brute beast devoid of reason, the Creator Himself hath evidently in some way made it known that its master is going to leave it." And saying this, the Saint blessed the work-horse, which turned away from him in sadness.

(In 1906 during the removal of an ancient entrenchment of the early monastery, the bones of a small horse were found carefully buried six feet deep in the hard stony embankment. The bones were restored to the earth, except for a tooth. It is not unlikely the remains were the white horse who bid farewell to his master Columba. There, a wayside cross was set up.)

Then leaving this spot, he ascended the hill that over-looketh the monastery, and stood for some little time on its summit; and as he stood there with both hands uplifted, he blessed his monastery, saying:

"Small and mean though this place is, yet it shall be held in great and unusual honor, not only by Scotic Kings and people, but also by rulers of foreign and barbarous nations and by their subjects: the Saints also even of other Churches shall regard it with no common reverence."

After these words he descended the hill, and having returned to the monastery sat in his hut transcribing the Psalter, and coming to that verse in the 33rd Psalm; where it is written, "They that seek the Lord shall want no manner of thing that is good" - "Here," said he, "at the end of the page, I must stop; and what follows let Baithene write." . . .

Having written the aforementioned verse at the end of the page, the Saint went to church on the nocturnal vigils of the Lord's Day; and so soon as this was over, he returned to his chamber, and spent the remainder of the night on his bed, where he had a bare flag for his couch and for his pillow a stone, which stands to this day as a kind of monument beside his grave. While he was reclining there, he gave his last instructions to the brethren, in the hearing of his attendant alone, saying: "These, O my children, are the last words I address to you - that ye be at peace, and have unfeigned charity among yourselves; and if you thus follow the example of the holy fathers, God, the Comforter of the good, will be your Helper, and I abiding with Him, will intercede for you; and He will not only give you sufficient to supply the wants of this present life, but will also bestow on you the good and eternal rewards which are laid up for those that keep His commandments." Thus far have the last words of our venerable patron, as he was about to leave this weary pilgrimage for his heavenly country, been preserved for recital in our brief narrative.

After these words, as the happy hour of his departure gradually approached, the Saint became silent. Then as soon as the bell tolled at midnight, he rose hastily, and went to the church; and running more quickly than the rest, he entered it alone, and knelt down in prayer beside the altar. At the same moment his attendant Diarmait, who more slowly followed him, saw from a distance that the whole interior of the church was filled with a heavenly light in the direction of the Saint. And as he drew near to the door, the same light which he had seen, and which was also seen by a few more of the brethren standing at a distance, quickly disappeared. Diarmait therefore, entering the church, cried out in a mournful voice. "Where art thou, father?" And feeling his way in the darkness, as the brethren had not yet brought in the lights, he found the Saint lying before the altar; and raising him up a little, he sat down beside him, and laid his holy head on his bosom. Meanwhile the rest of the monks ran in hastily in a body with their lights, and beholding their dying father, burst into lamentations. And the Saint, as we have been told by some who were present, even before his soul departed, opened wide his eyes and looked round him from side to side with a countenance full of wonderful joy and gladness, no doubt seeing the Holy Angels coming to meet him. Diarmait then raised the holy right hand of the Saint, that he might bless his assembled monks. And the venerable father himself moved his hand at the same time, as well as he was able - that, as he could not in words, while his soul was departing, he might at least, by the motion of his hand, be seen to bless his brethren. Having given them his holy benediction in this way, he immediately breathed his last. After his soul had left the tabernacle of the body, his face still continued ruddy and brightened in a wonderful way by his vision of the Angels, and that to such a degree that he had the appearance, not so much of one dead as of one alive and sleeping. Meanwhile the whole church resounded with loud lamentations of grief.

After Columba's death a wild wind storm arose which blew so violently for three days and nights that no boat could cross the Sound. The monks held the last services for their Abbot in the privacy of their own community – "the wind screaming over the frail roof of the church, the

great candles flickering in the salt draught, heart-broken monks singing out the Psalms of the Dead against the organ tones of Heaven . . . and in their dead Saint, clad in robes of his office, calm and peaceful with his fierce, passionate life in the Service of God left behind him forever."
(Shane - Isle of Columcille. p. 120)

The body of Columba lay in his tomb for over a hundred years before being transferred to a rich shrine of gold and silver, where it reposed for another two hundred years. During this time Iona was a place of pilgrimage for visitors from England, Scotland, Ireland and as far away as France. After the plundering raids of the Danes and Vikings began, ravages which had been foretold by Columba, the shrine was taken to Ireland. It was taken to and from there several times over the years as danger threatened the Iona community. Finally it was taken to Downs where the relics of St. Patrick and St. Brigid had already been laid. There is some doubt as to his last resting-place, but there is no doubt that his spirit dwells in Iona.

Dying Message to the Brethren of all the Churches of His Order.

"These, my last words, I commend unto you, O my children, that ye shall preserve among yourselves, unfeigned charity and mutual peace; and if ye observe this rule according to the example of the holy fathers, God, the Strengthener of the good, will help you; and I, dwelling with Him, will pray for you; and not only shall there be provided for you by Him the necessaries of the present life, but also there shall be given you the gifts of eternal good things prepared for them that keep the Divine commandments."

ALBAN
Orkney Isles
Caithness
Moray Firth
Lewis
Skye
Rum
Coll
Tiree
IONA
Mull
Colonsay
Jura
Islay
Kintyre
Rathlin
Arran
Inverness
NORTHERN PICTS
Loch Ness
Great Glen of Alban
R. Don
R. Dee
Aberdeen
SOUTHERN PICTS
Scone
R. Earn
R. Forth
Firth of Forth
Argyle
Dumbarton
Edinburgh
R. Clyde
R. Tweed
Lindisfarne (Holy I.)
NORTHUMBRIA (Angles)
STRATHCLYDE (Britons)
DALRIADA (Scots)
Firth of Clyde
GALLOWAY (Picts)
Roman Wall
R. Tyne
Solway Firth
Ireland
Isle of Man

COLUMBA THE KING-MAKER

When Columba appeared on the Dalriada scene as an exile and penitent, the fortunes of his kinsmen were in a critical state. Three years earlier, King Brude mac Maelchon of the Picts had marched an army against the colony of Scots from Ireland, and their Scottish King Gabhran had been killed. Gabhran had been succeeded by one Conall, great-grandson of King Fergus. Conall was denied the name of King and obliged to accept the humbler title of "Toshach" (Taoiseach - modern Irish) which signified that the state of Dalriada was tributary to Pictland. This rankled the pride of the Scotic race from Ireland.

Eleven years after Columba's arrival on Iona (A.D. 574) Conall died. There was rivalry for the succession and Columba intervened. Columba claimed the kingship for Aidan, the son of King Gabhran. Although Aidan was not the favored candidate, Columba's choice was accepted without opposition. It is probably that the Scotic colony accepted Aidan because it was endorsed with Columba's promise to lend his support for the re-establishment of restoration of the Scot's sovereign kingship.

King Brude of the Picts seemingly approved of Aidan being inaugurated as "King of Dalriada" by the Abbot of Iona. However, Columba was not satisfied with just the restoration of the kingship but wanted to exact revenge from the Pictish conquerors. With characteristic boldness, he "ordained" Aidan sovereign King of Dalriada.

Adamnan wrote that Columba seems to have been exalted with the belief that no consequences would follow from his act of ordination. "During the words of ordination," says Adamnan, "he (Columba) prophesied future events regarding Aidan's son, grandsons and great-grandsons, as he laid his hand upon his head and blessed him." It is noteworthy that in like manner Jacob blessed his son. It is not recorded, but it seems likely that the inauguration stone (Lia Fail) was used as a throne on this occasion as it was used by Scottish monarchs in succeeding generations.

Aidan's coronation proclaimed Dalriada's independence from Pictish rule and the Pictish monarch King Brude seems tacitly to have accepted the "fait accompli." It brought the Church and its influence into a unique alliance with the Scotic kingdom. By the laying-on of hands, Columba had signified that the ordination of a king was akin to religious ordination. He had invested secular authority with Christian sanctity.

During this time the rulers of Dalriada had their capital on the hillfort of Dunadd on the mainland of Argle, a lofty stronghold that rises over the meadows of Crinan Moss and gives a view of the Surgin Sound of Javan. In years to come, coronations would be there but Aidan traveled to Iona for his royal ceremony. Adamnan tells us that Columba was given a vision that Aidan should be "ordained to the kingship" in a particular manner. With much prayer and meditation he devised a ceremony rite that has been followed by successive monarchs of Scotland and Ireland.

The actual ceremony of Aidan is not fully described, however from later royal inaugurations in the Highland and the Isles, it is likely they originated from Columba's ceremony. On such occasions at Dunadd, when Aidan's successors were inaugurated king, we have the following description. "Near the summit of Dunadd, on a level surface of rock where the kings of Dalriada were crowned, a wild boar is incised in the rock here, and beside it the print of the human foot is carved out of the rock. The footmark is facing northeast. On the farther side of the figure of the boar is a circular hollow of 'ballan' in the rock. It is thought that the kings of Dalriada were crowned as they stood with the left foot forward and placed in the footmark, and that they were anointed with holy water taken from a natural font or stoup for the holy water." (Seton Gordon, op. cit.)

Another account of a Highland coronation may be cited by the same author. (Seton Gordon) When the great Clan Donald ruled the Isles as independent kings in the later Middle Ages, MacDonald was inaugurated on a certain coronation island in Loch Finlaggan within the island of Islay. Gordon wrote, "The ceremony took place . . . in the presence of a bishop, seven priests, and the chiefs and chieftains of all the leading Highland families. On the island was a square stone seven or eight feet long, and in this stone a hollow of the shape of a man's foot had been cut. Wearing a white robe, and with one foot in this hollow, MacDonald stood while a white rod was placed in one of his hands. This white staff was his pledge that he was to rule in a Christian manner, without tyranny or oppression. His father's sword was then placed in his other hand, and he was anointed by the bishop while those present offered their prayers for the new king."

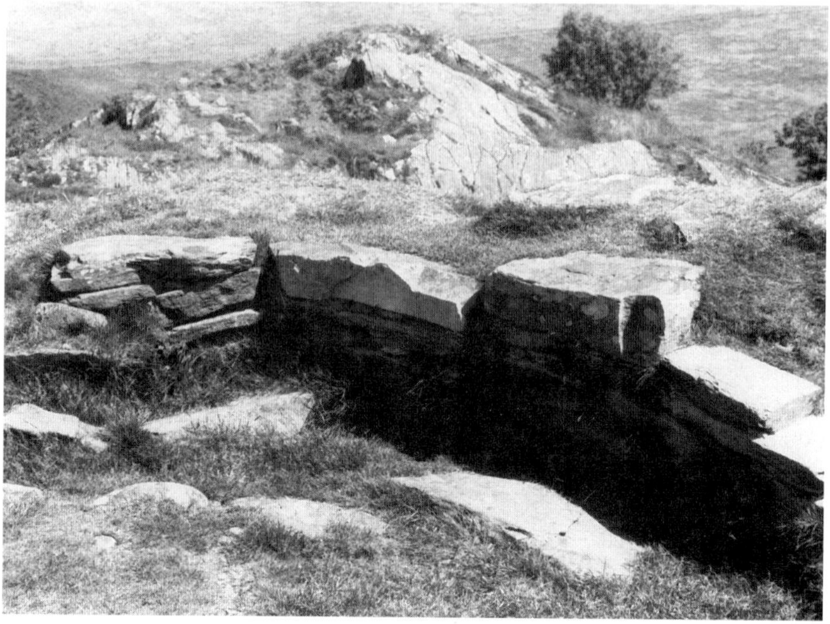

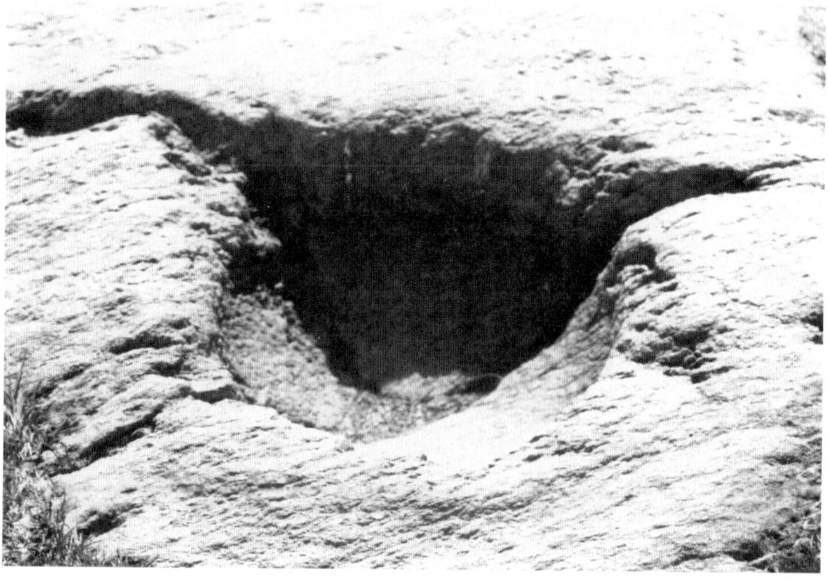

DUNADD FORT

DUNADD WAS THE CAPITAL OF THE SCOTS OF DALRIADA. OCCUPIED INTERMITTENTLY FROM THE 6TH-9TH CENTURIES A.D., IT IS AN OUTSTANDING EXAMPLE OF A DARK AGE FORTIFICATION. EVERY ADVANTAGE IS TAKEN OF NATURAL FEATURES BY STONE RAMPARTS WHICH FORM A SERIES OF DEFENSIVE ENCLOSURES EXTENDING FROM THE MAIN CITADEL ON THE SUMMIT. WITHIN THE ENCLOSURES STOOD THE TIMBER BUILDINGS OF THE INHABITANTS. NO TRACE OF THESE SURVIVES, BUT A BOAR OF PICTISH TYPE, AND A FOOT PRINT AND BASIN SUPPOSEDLY CONNECTED WITH THE INAUGURATION OF THE KINGS OF DALRIADA, ARE STILL VISIBLE CARVED IN THE ROCK NEAR THE TOP OF THE HILL.

The ceremony inauguration of King Aidan (in A.D. 574) has been called "the first royal coronation in Great Britain." All royal inaugurations of later times may be traced back to Columba's act, when on that spray-sprinkled island, within a little wooden church, the royal and consecrated hands of Columcille the abbot were laid on the head of Aidan of Dalriada, who was seated upon that mysterious and rugged coronation stone of destiny.

Dalriada was now declared a kingdom, with its sovereign seated in Alba, while part of Antrim, although in the Kingdom of Ireland, remained his. However, this posed a political problem. Was Irish Dalriada to be treated as separated from the High-Kingship of Ireland? Was Ireland to be partitioned? To decide this issue and two others which were facing the new High-King, Aidan, Aodh mac Ainmore of Ireland called a major convention (a Great Dail). Princes and chiefs and the heads of the clergy of Ireland were brought together at a green ridge named Drumceat (today Daisy Hill near the town of Limavady) in the High-King's patrimonial territory in Ulster.

To accommodate the visitors to the convention a sort of temporary town was constructed. Three issues were to be debated and decided. The first was to decide the status of the Irish Dalriada. The second was to consider a proposal to suppress or to banish the national order of guild of poets and jurists, which are loosely described as "the Bards". The third issue was an obscure dispute over the captivity of Scannlan mor, the son of the King of Ossory, who had appealed to Columba through the agency of the monastery of Durrow, which was in his kingdom.

Columba's arrival in Ireland was in violation of his resolve to forever banish himself from his native land, but his concern over the future of Dalriada was stronger. He was determined that the kingship of Adian be free and independent from Irish rule. Columba probably voyaged in his curragh from Iona, direct to Derry and his old monastic home. From there, with a retinue of clergy, he would have stated for the convention at Drumceat, not far from Derry. A contemporary poetic account says:

> "Forty priests was their number,
> Twenty bishops, noble, worthy,
> For singing psalms, a commendable usage
> Fifty deacons, thirty students."
> (The Historical Saint Columba – Simpson)

The remarkable number of 140 clergy would be no great exaggeration, since the "Family of Columcille" would number in the thousands from monasteries in two lands. The large number proportion of bishops is explained by the peculiarity of the Irish monasteries, in which, as a rule, the abbots were not bishops, but a number of holy monks sometimes were raised to the Episcopal dignity, without Episcopal functions.

In spite of his cool reception, Columba, as he entered the convention hall, was greeted by another son of the High-King, Domhnall, who rose and gave the great Abbot his place. What arguments were used and how long each issue was debated, we can only guess, but the long session of the "Mordhail" lasted for many months. The Gaelic nature does not favor a quick decision by a majority vote. An Irish historian wrote: "The Gael who goes into council is discontent if the ultimate decision is not unanimous. He is not satisfied until, after everybody has spoken and all minds have been opened, a course is found on which some unanimous decision can be enacted. This trait is found in every society, league, or deliberative assembly of Irishmen down to the present day. A majority decision irks; a united mind is what the Irish instinct craves, knowing that no settlement will be permanent unless it is an agreed settlement." (The Saints of Ireland - Blacam)

When the problem of Dalriada had been debated exhaustively, Aidan stating his case for a continued claim on the Irish part of Dalriada, and the High-King expounding his objections, it was decided to submit the issue to arbitration. A young churchman, one Colman mac

Comgallain, who evidently had won the confidence of the opposing parties by his devotion to fairness, was chosen as the arbitrator. Columba was pleased with the selection, having known and loved Colman as a youth. No doubt he felt Colman would be receptive to his wishes.

The settlement proposed by Colman and decided on was that the kingdom of Dalriada in Alba should be recognized as free from tribute and military levies, but Dalriada in Ireland should contribute military levies to the High-King. Each branch of the Dalriada, in Scotland and Ireland, should send ships to the other's aid in time of need. One effect of this settlement was that the Irish colony in Alba was recognized by Ireland as an independent kingdom. Ultimately, Scotland became a nation by the work of Columba.

The proposal to suppress or exile the Bards was defeated. In spite of the arrogance and exorbitant fees extracted from their patrons, Columba pleaded against the suppression of the Bardic order. He thought poets should be protected and their craft fostered. He is supposed to have argued that the wealth that kings and wealthy men give to poets is in things that perish, but the praises which poets give to kings and patrons are imperishable. "Fame lasts longer than jewels." (Is buaine bladh iona seoid) is a saying attributed to Columba. The affairs of Prince Scannlan's captivity was also settled to Columba's satisfaction. Scannlan was released.

Although Columba possessed a stormy passionate nature, quick to anger like many Celts, even to vindictiveness, he also was capable of intense compassion for human life. Although he could speak with the authority of royal birth, he could be terrible in his denunciation of sin, and of oppression of the poor. He had a deep affection for his own people but no desire to see them conquer or dominate others. His patriotism took the practical form of using his influence and energies to induce the Scots and the Picts to live side by side in mutual respect.

As the years progressed, Columba's "dove" nature subdued the vehemence of his lower nature by will-power, prayer and spiritual love. In his dealing with the political and religious leaders of pagan Scotland he relied on the power and efficacy of Divine Love to win them over to Christianity. Columba's greatest works took place in the quiet of his community on the Isle of Iona.

Celtic Scotland at time of Columba

COLUMBA THE MISSIONARY

Columba's objective was the conversion of Scotland, which he called "Alba of the Ravens." It must be noted that the political relationship between Columba and his Scotic countrymen and the Picts, which he is said to have evangelized, was not cordial. The Scots were immigrants from Ireland; squatters whose presence in Pictland was much resented. Modern writers, blissfully ignoring any consideration of the political circumstances of the time, describe Columba as wandering incessantly over the length and breadth of Scotland, mainland and islands included, founding hundreds of churches.

Adamnan writes of only five occasions where Columba had been beyond the "Dorsum Britanniae" (Drumalban) or central ridge of Scotland. Since the record is not chronological, it is not certain that these were separate occasions. A visit to Loch Ness was on a journey to King Brude in A.D. 564. However, this visit was probably more a political rather than a religious mission, having for its object the rehabilitation of his Dalriadic kinsmen whom King Brude had so badly mauled some years previously.

It has not gone unnoticed by some historians that Columba was a politician first and an ecclesiastic afterwards. He clearly identified himself, prominently and passionately, with the Scotic Kingdom. His steady championship of the Scots greatly restricted his freedom of access into the Pictland or the good will of the Pictish High King. After the smashing Pictish victory over the intrusive Scotic Kingdom it was fortunate for the Scotish Church that the Pictish nation that had their own organized church and tolerated their presence.

Although the venerable Bede (English historian of A.D. 672-735) implies that Columba converted King Brude, it is clear from Adamnan's narrative that in spite of the allegedly miraculous and dramatic success of the Saint's first interview with the Pictish monarch, the Druids were not dismissed from the King's court. Adamnan's statement that the Druids continued to exercise all their old influence over the King seems to decidedly outweight the later Bede, who had no access to Scotic records and had not even seen Adamnan's "Life of Columba." Nowhere does Adamnan state that Columba converted King Brude; he merely says the Pictish King held Columba in high honor.

It should be pointed out that had King Brude accepted Christianity from Columba, he would have allowed the Saint to establish a church in his capital. No such church has been found, and if it had been it is unlikely to have been forgotten, connected with so memorable an event. It is also quite possible that King Brude was already a Christian. In this early period of the Christian church, Druidism was merging into Christianity which would account for the Druids in the King's court. We know that King Brude's successor, Gartnaidh certainly was a Christian and, it is believed, founded a church at Abernathy. (Early Sources Vol. 1).

Scotic writers from Adamnan's time downward give prominence to Columba's visit to King Brude describing the negotiations with the Pictish king as being carried out by the Saint alone. They completely ignore his two distinguished Pictish companions. Adamnan mentions them as "companions" leaving the inference that they were some of Columba's disciples. However, the companions were in fact two of the most acclaimed saints of the period – Congall of Bangod and Cainnech of Achaboc. Both were Irish saints, and Columba probably thought their presence would materially aid his mission.

Why the influence of Columba's missionary endeavors was so greatly exaggerated in after ages, can be traced back to the facts of subsequent history. Out of the long struggle between the Scots of Dalriada and their unwilling hosts, the Picts, it was the Scots who emerged triumphant. Modern writers erroneously describe Columba as responsible for the conversion of Pictland. The facts are quite different. The Picts, long before Columba's time, had received the Gospel message from St. Ninian, who between the years 397 and 432 had established missions up the east coast of Scotland, probably as far as Shetland.

St. Ninian's central community was at Candida Case (the white house), and it was from there that missionaries carried on the evangelization of the Picts up to and after the Coming of Columba. St. Congall (the Great) and his deputy St. Moluag founded Christian communities throughout Pictland, ranging from Skye as far as Aberdeenshire, and even penetrated into the hostile territory of the Scots in Dalriada. About the very moment that Columba landed on Iona, Moluag was establishing a community of the Pictish Church almost next door to Iona, in the island of Lismore. The common assumption that the Picts in Columba's time were utterly uncivilized is entirely erroneous.

Tradition tells of a playful interchange between the Pictish Moluag and Columba the impetuous and impatient Gael. Perhaps jealous of Moluag's success at the island of Lismore, Columba is reported to have exclaimed. "May you have the alder for your firewood." Alder is bad fuel. "The Lord will make the alder burn pleasantly," replied the Pict, whose racial temperament was placid. "May you have the jagged ridges for your pathway!" cried Columcille. "The Lord will smooth them to my feet," placidly answered Moluag. (Historical Saint Columba - Simpson)

From Bangor of the Irish Picts, also in Columba's time, came St. Blaan who presided over the monastery founded by St. Catan at Kingarth in Bute. "Because this church was founded during the life-time of Columba, the church was subject to Iona" according to the historian Skene. (Celtic Scotland vol. II) However, it is upon such gratuitous assumption, repeated until it has usurped the weight of a fact, that current modern conceptions of Columba's influence in Pictland are largely based.

Modern historians are generally mistaken in the common assumption that the Picts, whose ancestors are the Cimmerians and kinsmen of the Celtic Scots, in Columba's time were still sunk in paganism. On the contrary, Christianity was already widely extended among them. (Early Sources, Vol. I - Anderson). It was a Christianity quite independent of and anterior in origin to the Scotic church based on Iona. The Pictish church, in fact, was based upon three main center: Candida Casa, Glasgow, and both of the Britons and Bangor of the Irish Picts. None of these had any organic connection whatsoever with the Iona community.

A critical examination of Columba's work brings out most strongly the fact that his apostolic labors were almost entirely restricted to his Scotic fellow-nationals of Dalriada, with whom his sympathies were completely bound up. The Pictish tribes Columba did evangelize were those on the Dalriadic frontier who came under the influence of the intrusive and dominating race. It is significant that Columba's genuine foundations nearly always bore the name "Kilcolimcille", the church of Columcille.

Columba founded fifty-three churches and monasteries of which traces have come down to us in the country we now call Scotland. Thirty-two of these were in the Western Isles and twenty-one in the

Northern country of Caledonia, which had been occupied by Picts. Many of these Picts had been won to Christ by St. Ninian, but after his death had lapsed into their former life and habits. It should be noted, that in his missionary endeavors, Columba, while following "Catholic" usages, allowed no supremacy to the Bishop of Rome. He knew no special cult of the Blessed Virgin Mary and the Infallibility of the "Pope". In short, he was not a Roman Catholic, and recognized nothing of the claims of modern Romanism.

After the accession of Kenneth Mac Alpin (half a Pict by blood but wholly a Scot by sympathy) in A.D. 843 to the combined throne of Dalriada and Pictland, the Scotic church came first to dominate and thereafter to absorb its Brito-Pictish predecessor. And with the extension of the Scotic church extended also the glory of its founder and patron saint, Columba. Moreover, even before the event of the coronation of Kenneth Mac Alpin, there were signs of weakening in the Pictish church. About A.D. 730, its illustrious parent, St. Ninian's monastery at Candida Casa, was absorbed by the English of Northunbria, and forthwith was reorganized on Roman lines. "From being the mother-church of the Britons and Picts it was degraded to be the church of a local diocese, subordinate to York," (Pictish Nation - Scott).

Although we cannot endow Columba with the sole credit for the evangelization of the country we now call Scotland, we must acknowledge the large share he bore of that noble work. Politically also his influence was of the utmost importance in the early history of the nation. He also consolidated and revived the oppressed kingdom of the Dalriada Scots that led to making it the culminating partner in the four principalities that eventually shared the soil of Alba. With the Scots rather than the Picts the future would lie, and no small share in the causes underlaying this momentous fact must be assigned to the personality of Columba. Throughout the thirty-four years of his residence at Iona, Columba was a steadfast champion of the Scotic intruders and a bitter foe of the Picts.

The old racial rivalry of some fifteen hundred years ago is now a dim and half-forgotten story. The blood of the Picts and Scots has long since mingled, and both justly hold Columba, even with all his faults, as one of the greatest and most outstanding figures of his day. His influence, though not in his own time, was profoundly exerted in the evangelization of England. From Iona, in the century after Columba's death, there came to the pagan Angles of Northumbria the great message of a purer faith, the "White Christ joining battle with Woden and Thor." (Historical Saint Columba-Simpson)

The Columbian Church produced the great missionary St. Aidan who in 635 became the Bishop of the Holy Island of Lindisfarne. Under his leadership the Northumbrian Church blossomed and counted many converts to Christianity. Its marvelous artistic achievement in sculpture and illuminated word, as illustrated by the Ruthwell Cross and the Linisfarne Gospels, are considered by some scholars of Scottish history as the brightest jewel in Columba's crown.

Saint Cuthbert   A.D. 634-687

ST. CUTHBERT'S CROSS

Saint Cuthbert was born c. 634 A.D., and even as a boy seemed to be destined for high office. One night when a young man, Cuthbert was out on the hillside keeping sheep. Whilst at his prayers he suddenly saw a great light and a choir of angels descending to earth. They took back with them "a soul of exceeding brightness". Next day Cuthbert learned that Aidan, Bishop of Lindisfarne, had died the previous night, and he immediately decided to become a monk.

Cuthbert spent many of his early years at Melrose, undertaking long missionary journeys. Following the synod of Whitby in 664, Eata, Abbot of Melrose, moved to Lindisfarne, taking Cuthbert with him. Cuthbert continued his missionary work, but longed for more time to devote to meditation and prayer. In 676 he retired to the inhospitable Farne Islands and there made his cell. Cuthbert refused a bishopric many times, but in 685 agreed to become Bishop of Lindisfarne. Immediately after Christmas 686 Cuthbert returned to his hermitage on Farne Island, and there he died on 20th March, 687. His body was taken to Lindisfarne. After many raids by the Danes the monks fled, taking Cuthbert's body with them. After years of wandering their successors eventually brought it to Durham in 995, and commenced building the first Cathedral. St. Cuthbert's tomb is still in Durham Cathedral, behind the High Altar.

LATER HISTORY OF IONA

After the death of Columba in 597, the Celtic Church (as all these churches were called) continued and spread. The Iona monks traveled to England and the Continent with their message of Christ's love and the need for fellowship among men. As they went forth the monastery of Iona trained others and sent them forth, so that Iona's power and influence spread far beyond the bounds of Scotland. It was the Columban monks who built the first great monastery at Lindisfarne that became a second Iona and the well-spring of Christianity in Northern England.

The Columban monks made Christ's name known in Germany and Switzerland, and under these Irish teachers the spirit of racial bitterness was checked. A new intercourse sprang up between English, Picts, Britons and Irish. They sought out and trained simple, earnest men who desired to live only to preach the Gospel and the love of Christ. That was the foundation on which they built up the Church of Northumbria.

By A.D. 814, the Iona monastery, so depleted and looted, could no longer hold its position as the organizing center of the Scottish Church, and the primacy was transferred temporarily to Kells, in Ireland. The Iona monks, however, clung to their island home and bravely proceeded to build a new monastery of stone and on a better site where the restored Abbey Church now stands.

The plan of the new monastery seems to have been that of several small churches clustered together. Sometimes the monks had simultaneous services in all these churches, or perhaps alternating so that there was always a continuous round of services, day and night. It is believed the chief Church was the one now standing to the northeast of the present Abbey.

Shortly after this time King Brian Boru of Ireland subdued the Irish Danes and Iona suffered no more from them. However, the primacy did not go back to Iona, but passed to Dunkeld, where Constantine, King of the Picts had erected a monastery far from the danger zone. From there it was moved to Abernathy and finally in 908 to St. Andrews. In Iona the office of Abbot was succeeded by that of Coarb of Columkill (heir of Columba) and held usually by the Abbot of one of the greater Irish monasteries who ruled Iona from afar. Iona, like the Culdee Church, steadily declined in importance.

Following the turbulent ninth century, there came a long period of relative peace. Although the Danish invaders had been succeeded by the Norse Vikings, they apparently were not aggressive toward Iona. During the rest of the Culdee Church period, the possession of the Western Isles fluctuated between Scotland and Norway. In 1097, King Magnus of Norway (called Magnus Barelegs because of his adoption of the kilt during his fighting in the Hebrides) came ashore to do homage to the Isle of Columba. For the next sixty-five years nothing more is heard of Iona until a notice appeared in the annuals of Ulster of a deputation to Ireland in 1164.

In the eleventh century, Iona passed into the Diocese of Man and the isles which had been created by the Norwegian conquerors. In 1154 the See was put under the Archbishop of Trondjem in Norway, and remained there until 1266, when the Hebrides were finally ceded to Scotland and the primacy moved back to Dunkeld. The twelfth century saw the complete Latinization of the Scottish Church. Iona, owing to her isolated position, escaped the longest, but early in the thirteenth century, Reginald, son and heir of the great Somerled, "lord of the Isles", established a monastery of Benedictines on the island. Shortly afterwards, Reginald established a community of nuns of the same order and placed his sister Beatrice as its first Prioress.

The Benedictine occupation of Iona was uneventful and in 1204 another monastery was erected by Cellach. At this time the last of the Columbian monks into the Hebrides apparently never molested Iona. The marriage of Malcolm Canmore, son of Duncan and successor to Macbeth on the Scottish throne, with Margaret, a Saxon princess, who with her family had taken refuge in Scotland after the Norman Conquest, marked the downfall of the Culdee or Celtic Church. Margaret was a thorough Saxon and devout member of the Roman Church which held rule over the Anglian Church. She was instrumental in the supersession at Court of the Gaelic tongue by "Scottis" or Scots, derived from the Anglian settlers in the Lothians.

Margaret was genuinely distressed to find, in the land of her adoption what she considered errors in the observance of Lent; neglect of the Sunday holy day and "Masses in I know not what barbarous rite." A woman of great piety and zeal, she "restored the monastery of Hy, which Columba, the servant of Christ, had erected in the time of Brude, son of

Meilcon, King of Picts. It had fallen into ruin in the storms of war and the lapse of ages, but the faithful queen rebuilt and restored it, and gave the monks an endowment for the performance of the Lord's work." (Ordericu Vitgalis)

After the restoration of Iona, Margaret set herself wholeheartedly to the task of Latinizing the Scottish Church. After a Celtic reaction, this policy was continued by her third son, David I, who abolished the Celtic liturgy. He organized regular dioceses, administered by bishops and parish priests, and replaced the Culdee (Celtic) monks with Benedictine monks and Augustinian canons. By the end of his reign, practically all the medieval sees had been founded.

In 1549 Donald Monro (Dean of the Isles) visited Iona and from him we have a picture of the island twelve years before the Reformation, when the community was swept into exile. Monro wrote: "Within this ile there is a monastery of monckes, and one of the nuns, with a paroche-kirke, and sundrie uther chapels, dotat of aud by the Kings of Scotland and by Clandonald of the iyles."

At the time of the Reformation in 1560, all the island and the Monastery passed into the hands of Maclean of Duart. Seemingly no attempt was made to destroy the buildings. Later in 1609, Andrew Knox, who was Bishop of the Isles in the temporary episcopate established a year later, held a convention of several chiefs of the Highlands and islands, on Iona. Here the "Statutes of Icolkill" were drawn up and subscribed to, the chiefs pledging themselves to repair the churches throughout their territories, to provide parish ministers, to promote the observation of the Sabbath day, and to endeavor to put a stop to certain undesirable practices which were then prevalent.

In 1617 the Abbey of Iona was annexed to the Bishopric of the Isles. Eighteen years later, Charles I wrote to Maclean of Duart asking him to restore the Island of Icolmkill to the Bishop, and in the same year ordered the Lords of the Exchequer to pay to the Bishop the sum of 400 pounds for the restoration of the Abbey Church. However, this grant was evidently never made, for when Sacheverell, Governor of Man visited Iona in 1688, the buildings were still in ruins, Sacheverell wrote: "Though they have no minister, they constantly assemble in the great church on Sundays, where they spend most of the day in private devotions."

In 1693 Iona passed from the Macleans to the Campbells, under their chief the Duke of Argyll. In 1894 an Episcopal chapel was consecrated in the newly built "St. Columba's House", known locally as the Bishop's House. Later a library was added and in a studio in the village of Iona, old Celtic design articles of wood, brass and silver jewelry were produced. In 1899 the eighth Duke of Argyll deeded (gift) the Abbey Church and all other ecclesiastical buildings on the Island to the Church of Scotland.

In 1900 the Church of Scotland restored the Abbey itself, but the other buildings remained in ruins. Shortly after 1938 the Iona Community was established by Reverend George F. Macleod, which was integrated by the General Assembly of the Church of Scotland into full fellowship in the Church. The community took on the responsibility of restoring the other ecclesiastical buildings of Iona.

Like the monks of old, the community members have a "Rule of Life", which they promise to follow. It consists of daily prayer, Bible study, planning each day and accounting for money spent. After a period of training on the island they move back to the mainland to teach in churches, in the slums, factories, dockyards and new housing areas, that religion and life must travel hand in hand. And most importantly, Christ must be a part of each person's daily life.

Michael Chapel and Museum

THE CULDEE CHURCH

In the same century which saw the establishment of the simple community on Iona by the followers of St. Columba, the throne in the Vatican at Rome was occupied by a man with a very different character from Columba's. Elected Pope in 590 A.D., Gregory the Great was an administrative genius who, more than anyone else, was responsible for creating the Church of Rome in the form that we know today. A former Roman magistrate of great wealth, he modeled his Church in a considerable extent on the empire of the Caesars, using military power to defend and consolidate his dominion.

Gregory saw the Culdee (Celtic) Church as the most serious obstacle to the expansion of the authority of Rome. Earlier in his ecclesiastic career, Gregory himself had undertaken a mission to Britain to proselytize the inhabitants, but was ordered home by the then Pope. However, when he became Pope he passed the mission on to Augustine, prior to the Benedictine monastery he had founded in his former palace at Rome.

Augustine landed in Kent in the year of the death of Columba, 597 A.D. With thirty monks and banners and chanting litanies, they marched to Canterbury, the capital of the King of Kent, Aethelbert. Augustine was granted a dwelling-place for his monks and the liberty to preach. That same year Aethelbert allowed himself to be baptized and several thousand of his chieftains and nobles followed his example. Although Augustine was given authority over the Culdee Churches in Britain, his mission had little immediate success. He approached the leaders of the Culdee Church in Wales, but his efforts to induce them to submit to Rome were rejected with scorn.

At a meeting, somewhere in the area of the River Severn, the Culdee bishops confronted Augustine. It is noted that Augustine lacked the courtesy to rise and greet them. According to the historian, Geoffrey of Monmouth, the Culdee bishops, when asked to defer to the authority of Rome, replied:

"We know no other Master than Christ. We know nothing of the Bishop of Rome in his new character as Pope. We like not his new-fangaled customs. We are the British Church, the Archbishop of which is accountable to God alone, having no superior on Earth. Be it known and declared, that we all, individually and collectively, are in all humility prepared to defer to the Church of God, and to its Bishop of Rome, and to every sincere and Godly Christian so far as to love everyone to his degree in perfect charity, and to assist them all by word and deed in becoming the children of God.

"But as for any other obedience we know of none that he whom you term 'the Pope', or 'Bishop of Bishops' can demand. The deference we have mentioned we are ready to pay to him as to every other Christian, but in all other respects our obedience is due to the jurisdiction of the Bishop of Caerleen, who is alone, under God, our ruler to keep us right in the way of salvation."

[According to Welsh tradition these are the Bishops who disputed with Augustine: (1) The Bishop of Caerfawydd, called Hereford; (2) The Bishop of Teillo; (Llandaff) (3) The Bishop of Llanbadarn Fawr; (4) The Bishop of Bangor; (5) The Bishop of Llanelwy; (St. Asaph) (6) The Bishop of Wegg; (7) The Bishop of Morganwg. (Haddan and Stubbs, Vol. III, pg. 41)]

While the Culdee Church did not object to the Roman Church doctrines in general, they rejected the confessional requirement of Rome as well as the authoritative absolution; and confessed to God alone, as believing God alone could forgive sins. There was also the controversy centered around the right method of calculating the date of Easter, and the form the tonsure (shaved portion of the head) should take. The fixing of the date of Easter was important because the rest of the Church's year was geared to it.

The Venerable Bede, in writing of the difference between the Scottish Church and the Church of Rome made mention of Easter being celebrated by the Scots, as well as the whole of the Pictish nation, from the fourteenth to the twentieth moon instead of the date that the Church of Rome had adopted in A.D. 463. The computation used by the British Church was believed to have been derived from the East, from the Apostle John himself.

The Culdee Church not only kept Easter at a different time from the Roman Church, they further marked themselves out by the different hair cut they had adopted. It is possible that the Culdee form of tonsure had been copied from the Druids. They shaved the front of the head from ear to ear, probably, however, leaving an encircling fringe across the forehead. When Adamnan returned to Iona after visiting Rome with a different hair clip, it resulted in a schism in the island monastery there. The monks who would not accept Adamnan's ruling, walked out and settled themselves in another part of Iona. Thereafter, until A.D. 767, there existed two monasteries on Iona.

Bede also reported that baptism by immersion in any water was the practice of the Scottish Church. "Without the ceremonies used by the Romanists, they (Culdees) baptized in any water they came to." This is confirmed by the complaint which Lanfrance, Archbishop of Canterbury, makes concerning the Irish Christians who were taught by the Culdees." "Infants are baptized by immersion, without the consecrated chrism." (consecrated oil) Seemingly consecration of infants was not in use.

The Liturgy of the Culdee Church differed from the Liturgy of the Church of Rome. This is revealed by Gregory's reply to Augustine's celebrated letter asking advice touching on certain points of inquiry. One question was what course he (Augustine) ought to pursue in reference to the Gallician Liturgy, which although different from the Roman, was in use in the British and Gallic Churches. (Bede, Eccles. Hist., I c 21)

In reply, Gregory told Augustine that he had nothing to do with the Bishop of Gaul, who was subject to the Bishop of Arles, but that he ought to have authority over the British Bishops; and that, in reference to the Liturgy, he ought to adopt that which would be most acceptable to the Saxon Church. (Bede, 1, 27) There existed at the time four great Liturgies, which had come down from the primitive church, and were the original sources from which all other were derived. These were known as the Liturgies of St. James, St. John, St. Peter, and St. Mark. The Liturgy of St. John was the one used by the Culdee Church and also by the Western Europe and Ephesine Churches.

Bede positively affirms that "John the Evangelist first chanted the Gallican course, then afterwards the blessed Polycarp, disciple of St. John, and then thirdly, Irenaeus, who was Bishop of Lyons, in Gaul, chanted the same course in Gaul." (Spelman, 'concila' Tom. I. P. 176) It is quite possible that Aristobulus, one of the "seventy" appointed by Jesus, carried the ecclesiastic rites of the Eastern Church when he went to Britain several centuries earlier. Aristobulus was martyred in Britain in A.D. 58 or 59. (Alrod, Regia, Fides, p. 41 - quoted in "Dedicated Disciples", Stough)

The policy of Augustine was to undermine the simplicity of worship among the Culdee (British Celtic) Church and to work on the imaginations of the wonder-loving Saxons by means of gaudy rituals and enticing doctrines which he imported from Italy. The worship of images, the flames of purgatory, the attainment of salvation from good works, the virtue of relics were among the instruments he employed. Augustine success with the Saxons pleased Gregory and in a letter to Ethelbert, he exhorted him to assist "Augustine in his good work by all the expedients of exhortation, terror, and correction." The Church of Rome was soon to exhibit her tender mercies of "terror and correction" toward the inhabitants of Britain who would not embrace Rome.

The elements of controversy between the Culdee and the Church of Rome, were in themselves trivial to the Culdees. It mattered little to them on what day they began to celebrate a feast, which had no divine authority in the Christian Church. Also, in what manner they practiced a tonsure, which had no better origin than the blind superstition of the priests of heathenism. The paramount question was, whether any church or bishop had a right to prescribe to all who bore the Christian name.

The Culdee Church, it would appear, withstood the idolatrous worship of the Roman Church. They vigorously opposed its errors, and resisted in encroachments into their affairs. The doctrine of the Culdee Church was comparatively pure scripture. According to Bede, they would only accept those things found in the writings of the prophets, evangelists and apostles. "They lived after the example of the venerable fathers . . . they lived by the labour of their hands."

The mode of life for the Culdees was quite different from the so-called monks of later years, who interpreted the Scriptures in a sense which it was never meant to bear, retiring singly to solitude and caves. Neither was celibacy the rule among the Culdees. However, the Culdees at St. Andrews who had wives, after entering into their monastic establishment, were not permitted to keep their wives in their houses.

Gifts received by the Culdees were immediately distributed with the greatest of cheerfulness to the poor who came their way. We know that while they held some things in common, their wives and children, or their nearest relations, after the death of any of them could claim and divide the deceased's property. This was mentioned by a Romish writer as regrettable. This indicates that the Culdees had no interest in aggrandizing their order, or of enriching the particular monasteries belonging to it, as was done by monastic bodies of subsequent ages.

The Culdee Church dedicated their principal churches to the "Holy Trinity" and not to the Blessed Virgin, or any Saint. This tallies with the account of John Toland (A.D. 1670-1722) of the Irish, while under the religious direction of the Culdees, ". . . in their public worship, they made an honorable mention of holy persons deceased; offering a sacrifice of thanksgiving for their exemplary life and death, but not by way of propitiation for sins."

The religion of the Culdee Church can best be stated as being in many circumstances connected with Druidic philosophy, a philosophy that found complete fulfillment in Christ. In Columba's own words; "Christ is my Druid." They owed no rule but the Word of God. They had no worship of saints or angels, no prayers for the dead, no confession to a priest, no elevation of Mary the mother of Jesus - all these practices were added later when Rome gained complete control of the Culdee Church.

The early Culdee Church and for several generations resisted the theological dictates of the Church of Rome. Although it is noticeable in history that the Church of Rome, conjoining policy with her power, attacked the Culdees for their failure to abide its dictates. The object of that Church was far more extensive. The Church of Rome was resolved to accomplish either the total extinction of the Culdee Church or their complete subjugation.

The extent to which the Church of Rome went to in order to dominate the Culdee Church can be seen in the writings of Bede describing Augustine striving to conform the Scottish and British churches to the Roman rites and to have himself acknowledged as the only Archbishop of Britain. He wrote: "After divers conferences, and much pains taken by him to persuade the Britains into conformity, when he could not prevail, he made offer, that, if they would yield to minister baptism, and observe Easter according to the Roman manner, and be assisting to him in reforming the Saxons, for all other things they should be left to their ancient customs. But they refusing to make any alteration, he (Augustine) fell a threatening, and said, 'they who would not have peace with their brethren, should finde warre with their enemies.' This falling out, as he foretold (for Edelfrid, King of Northumberland, invading them with a strong army, slew at one time 1200 monks that were assembled to pray for the safety of their countrymen) made Augustine to be suspected of the murder, and did purchase him a great deal of hatred; whether he foreknew the practice or not, is uncertain, but shortly after the murder of these monks, he himself died."

The monks referred to were chiefly those of Bangor, in Wales. Their abbot Dinoth was sacrificed with them. Bede represents this calamity as the effect of the prophecy delivered by the pious Augustine. But there is ever reason to believe that the prediction was founded on a predetermined plan. It is more probable that Augustine having taken council with King Ethelbert, not only knew of the war, but was himself the cause of it. For he was a close friend of that king who in turn persuaded Edelfrid to bring about the destruction of the Britain. It is also asserted that Augustine met with the kings at Caer-leon, when preparing for that battle.

Later, Roman writers, in order to exculpate Augustine, have attempted to show that he was dead before this battle was fought, but there is no confirmation of this theory in the writings of Bede's history. Further, the older Saxon accounts of the battle are silent on the matter. This gives reason to believe that Augustine's death before the battle was an interpolation made at that time of Alfred the Great. A Friar Minorite, Amandus Xierixiensis of Spain, states that "this war was raised against the Britons on account of their disobedience to St. Augustine; because the Saxons, who had been converted to Christianity, were resolved to subject the Britons to his authority."

The controversy between the two churches (Culdee and Roman) came to a head in A.D. 66 when a council met at Whitby to settle the differences. The English St. Wilfred championed the Roman case and prevailed. The Culdee Bishop Colman resigned his see and retired to Ireland leaving Wilfred to replace the Scotic churchmen with scholars favorable to Rome. The decision of 662 was far-reaching in its effects. It removed the direct Irish influence from northern England. York now replaced Lindisfarne as the spiritual capital of the northern English.

However, a body of Celtic ecclesiastics can be traced down to the fourteenth century. The Church in Wales did not recognize the Roman archbishop of Canterbury till the year A.D. 1115. Then took place a union between the Welsh and the now Romanized English churches, which prepared the way for the union of Wales with England. Even in this recognition, the Welsh Church denied the right of the Pope in Rome to interfere with their affairs.

In its lifetime the Culdee Church played a considerable part in preserving and developing Western culture at a time when Rome sought to subject the Western Church to a foreign yoke. The Scottish monasteries of Iona and Lindisfarne were great spiritual and intellectual centers sending Christian missionaries far afield; St. Fursa to Peronne, St. Fiarchre to Meaux, St. Killian to Warburg, and others as far as Italy and the Ukraine.

The Culdees established churches, monasteries and colleges, chiefly in remote places, where they fled to escape the persecution by the Roman Church. Many saints of the Culdee Church were at a later date claimed by the Roman Church; these saints owed nothing to Rome in connection with their conversion, and long struggled against her pretensions. Roman historians falsely claim these Culdee saints as though they had been her more devoted adherents. This is especially noticeable in the case of St. Patrick whose conversion was the result of training in a British home; who was all his life a Culdee, yet is now given the greatest prominence in Roman Catholic hagiology.

It should be noted that Roman monkish chronicles have done their best to bury the true story of the Culdee Church and their leaders whom we call saints. The records of these simple Celtic evangelists have been distorted or perverted, and in some cases, wholly expunged from their records. Admittedly, the written evidence of them is sparse and sometimes unreliable, because most of them were written five centuries after the events described, although some were no doubt based on earlier writings.

Historical truth was not always the primary objective of the chronicles. Often their stories were for the edification or glorification of the saintly founders of their monasteries. Hence, we find "miracles" ascribed to the saints, often borrowed from the lives of other saints or completely fictitious. However, they are not valueless as evidence.

They provide place-names of villages and farms, often named after the first missionaries to arrive, and the names of saints given to churches.

The Culdee Church left its mark on England to this day. Those "Catholics" of Columba's Gaelic tradition were attached to patriotism and conservation, the love of olden institutions which gave the nation its stability. Columban monks build their churches in wood, which became patterns for English hands to build in stone. From the Columban tutelage, northern English houses of religion reared the Venerable St. Bede, first and most English of English historians (to whom we owe most of our knowledge of these times) and Caedmon, first of the English poets and maker of hymns. English saints like Cedd and Chad were educated by the Scots, and founded English Sees. The great abbeys of Melrose, Whitby and St. Bee's rose in what Bede terms "the thirty years episcopate of the Scots" - the thirty most fruitful years in English history.

AERIAL VIEW OF MELROSE ABBEY FROM THE SOUTHEAST

IONA MONASTERY (ABBEY) TODAY

The present Abbey Church of Iona is a restoration of the church erected by Reginald Macdonald in A.D. 1203 which is believed to have been situated about 200 yards south of the site of the original wattle and daub buildings of Columba and his followers. Reginald's church was originally an Abbey, but in A.D. 1507 became the Cathedral of the Diocese of the Isles. It remained a Cathedral until the Reformation in 1560 when Protestantism was adopted by the Scottish Church.

Although only fragments remain of the Abbey founded by Reginald, later additions and restorations have been harmonious even though they have been spread over many centuries. Much of what one sees today is restorations of 1420 when the Abbey had to be rebuilt after over fifty years of neglect under the abbey of Fingon Mackinnon. The tower and the choir were completely remodeled at this time.

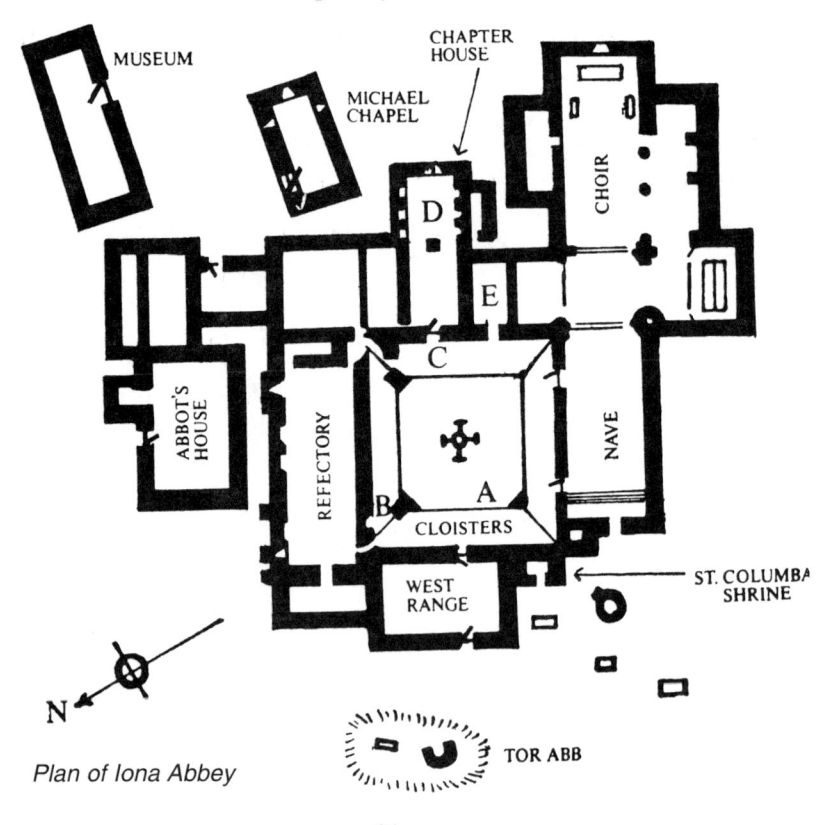

Plan of Iona Abbey

THE ABBEY

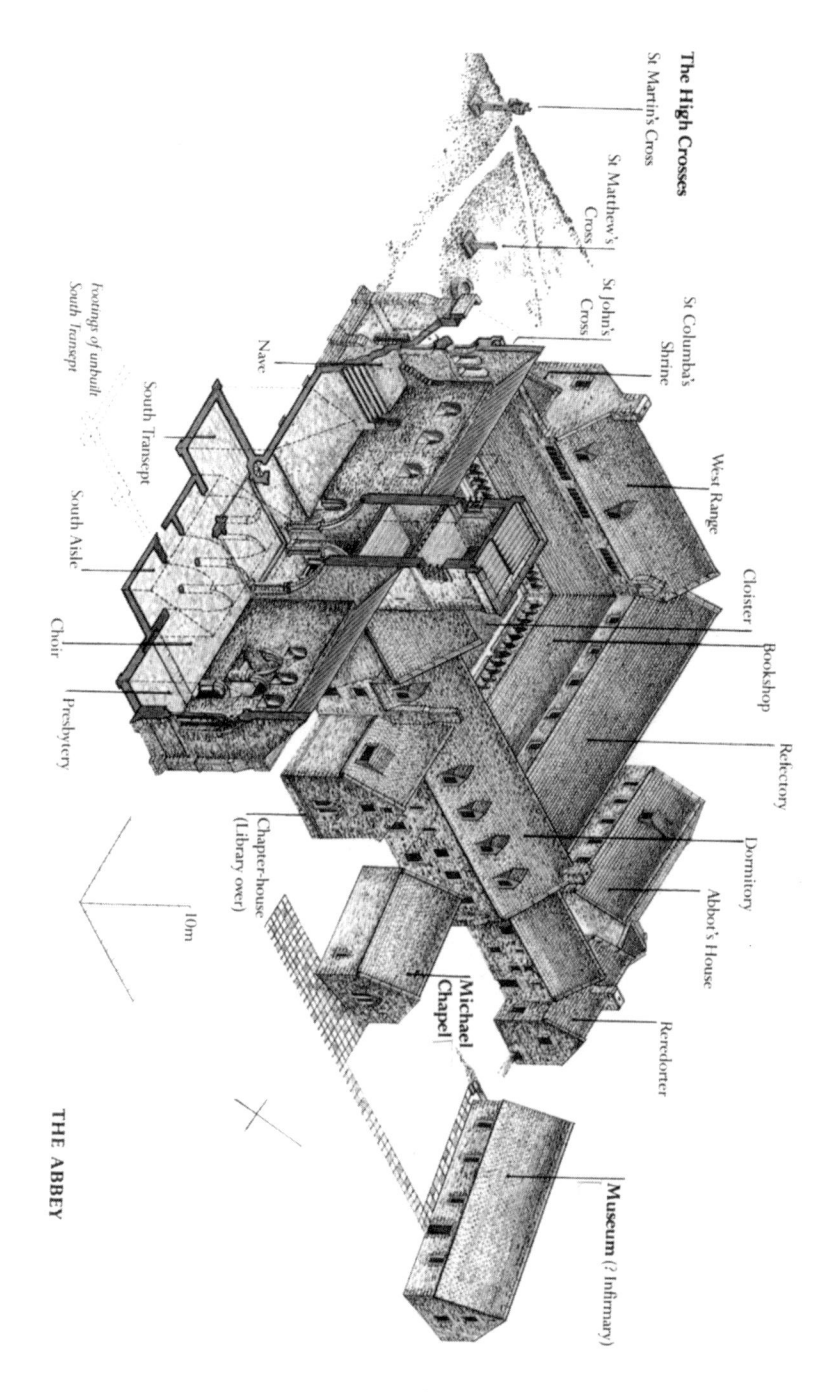

The building is cruciform in design, measuring 148 feet seven inches from east to west and 70 feet three inches from north to south. Though there are traces of late Norman alterations, most of the building dates from the fifteenth and early sixteenth century reconstructions. There are some traces of an earlier church but they are of a much later date than Columba.

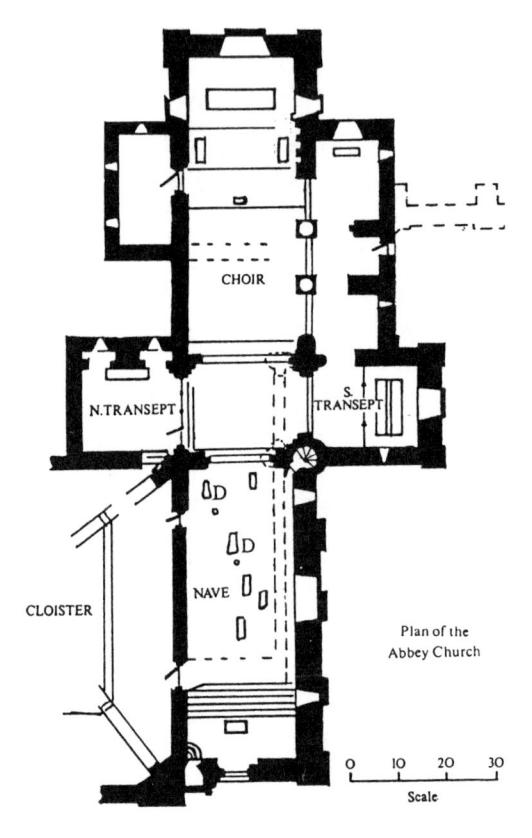

Plan of the Abbey Church

Today one enters the Abbey by the west door into the Nave, a part of the church reserved for the lay people. Beyond the Nave is the Choir for the ordained inmates of the monastery. From the Nave is the sacristy door dating from the fifteenth century, leading into the vestry where the priests would robe themselves before the services. Before 1500 the Choir floor was level with the base of the high arches above the door with a crypt beneath. At that date the crypt was removed and the present elaborate doorway formed.

The Sacristy Doorway

The Choir dates largely from the early sixteenth century re-building and was the first portion of the Abbey to be re-roofed. On either side are effigies of abbots. On the south Kenneth Mackenzie and on the north John Mackinnon who died in 1499. He was the last abbot of Iona to wear a mitre, a privilege granted to the abbots of Iona by Pope Innocent IV in 1247.

Effigy of Abbot Mackenzie

The south choir aisle dates from 1500 and is notable for its curious construction. The carvings of the capitals of the pillars are of great interest depicting among other subjects the Crucifixion and an angel weighing souls, with a devil depressing one side of the scale. Outside the south aisle are the foundations of a larger transept which was discovered some years ago. Also in the south transept are the marble effigies of the eight Duke of Argyll (d. 1900) and the Duchess Ina (Ina d. 1925 and buried beneath).

Two scenes from the capitals of the arches to the south choir aisle

The Fall – angel with the flaming sword

Attempted theft of a cow

In the floor of the Nave can be seen the remains of stone coffins cemented into the floor. When they were discovered and opened, there was found a "clutch" of stones in each one. It is thought they might represent the number of years the monk buried therein had spent at the monastery. The tombs were placed in the floor at the time of the restoration of the Abbey by the eight Duke of Argyll in 1899.

In the archway opposite the pulpit there is a carving of an ugly little face, evidently in pain and torment, just where it can be seen by the preacher. Evidently the monks put it there to encourage the preacher to do his best, by his preaching, to save the souls of his listeners from punishment.

Other details of interest within the church are carvings with curious medley of subjects; foliage, grotesque figures, groups of men and beasts, and Biblical subjects. The altar or Communion table at the east of the church is made of Iona marble from a quarry on the south side of the island.

The east wall in the north transept is the earliest part of the Church and dates from the thirteenth century. It was restored in 1905 and the beautiful rose window inserted. The two recesses by the windows formerly contained altars and the arch between contained a statue of which only the base remains. The windows of the Abbey are considered the finest of their kind in Britain or Europe. They differ in design. The one in the south wall of the transept is of a Celtic pattern and above it is the figure of a lamb and a cross in a pattern long identified with Joseph of Arimathea at Glastonbury.

The cloisters of the Abbey are situated on the north side of the church and on the west side of it are the remains of two medieval arches. The cloisters were restored in 1954 to match the two cloisters' arches existing from the restoration by Margaret Canmore. In the center of the cloisters is a statue entitled "The Descent of the Spirit".

Restored Cloisters

The Descent of the Spirit

The tower at the crossing of the church was formerly capped by a gabled roof containing a dovecote, and in the south belfry window is a medieval clock face. The hands of the clock were replaced in 1940. The bell in the belfry was a gift and installed in 1931. It was wrought by a Dutchman in 1510. The bell was found on a farm house in Hertfordshire, England, and believed to once have hung in the old Houses of Parliament in London.

South Side Abbey

West Side Abbey

St. Columba's Shrine

Columba's Pillow

THE NUNNERY

Like the Monastery, the Nunnery was established at the beginning of the thirteenth century by Reginald, Lord of the Isles. The architecture is Norman, of a type commonly used prior to the twelfth century. The stone used in its construction was blocks of pink granite from Eileen Nam Ban and the Ross of Mull. Visitors of the 17th and 18th centuries describe the Nunnery and furnish us with drawings of the remains. These drawings of the ruins show that by the 1760s little more survived than at present, with the exception of the chancel of the church which was roofed over.

About 1830 the roof collapsed and some repairs were done in 1874-1875 by the eight Duke of Argyll. After years of neglect it was decided in 1923 to make some repairs on the Nunnery but to forgo any restoration. This work was confined to the repair of the north chapel and sacristy and the planting of a garden within the cloisters.

The ruins today consist of the single-bay chancel, a nave and aisle of three bays and a north aisle-chapel above which is a small chamber, probably designed as a sacristy. The apartments grouped around the enclosure include a chapter-house with stone seats, a refectory (dining hall) and a kitchen in the south.

All the gravestones in the Nunnery mark the burying place of women, and many have lovely tracery and foliage. One stone has a carving of a comb and mirror on it and marks the grave of Prioress Anna who was the last Prioress. North of the Nunnery church is St. Roman's Chapel. For a long time this was the Parish Church for the island. It was roofed recently and contains some beautiful stones gathered from the ruined Nunnery to preserve them from wind and weather.

Nunnery Chapel

Nunnery

St. Finnan's Bell on St. Finnan's Island (Eilean Fhianain), Loch Shiel: a Celtic hand bell still preserved at the Celtic Church site with which it was associated

TOR ABB

Just west and overlooking the Iona Abbey is a small hillock where can be seen the remains of Columba's hut or cell. The Stone slab crowning the hill contains a slot for a small wood or stone cross erected shortly after the death of Columba to mark the site of his cell. Beside it slightly to the south one can see a circle of bluish stones fashioned with an adze. These stones are the remains of what would have been four to five foot high walls domed by wood or thatch covered by turf and heather.

100

A slanting whitish-grey rock would be Columba's couch. What looks like an open-air fireplace was in fact his seat. A wooden board would have extended across the two granite ends. The space under the board is where he could have kept his pigments for his writing. There would have probably been a flight of steps leading down to the Church. The cell would have looked like a small thatched cottage.

Columba was sitting in his cell inscribing the Psalms on the June night he died. It is recorded he had completed verse 10 of Psalms 34, "The young lions do lack and suffer hunger; but they that seek the Lord shall not want any good thing," when he laid down his pen, went down to the little church where he prayed and there he died in 597 A.D. The small chapel behind St. Martin's Cross is the site of his original tomb.

Today the chapel is called St. Columba's Shrine. Belonging to the Celtic period, it contained a small altar and on either side a stone shelf with a damask cloth upon each. On the left would be a bone of the Saint encrusted in jewels. On the right would lie his Bible, his staff and his bell. The Bible was the Vicar of Christ for the Celtic Church. The mission was shepherding and they could not be secretive. The Gospel Message must ring out loud.

THE ABBEY WELL

At the entrance to the west door of the Iona Abbey is a well which once was the base of a round tower. During the period between the 9th and 11th centuries A.D. the monasteries and farm dwellings of Scotland and Ireland suffered constant attacks by Scandinavian raiders who plundered anything of value which they could find in addition to terrorizing the inhabitants. So it became a common event for the monks to gather together their books and other valuables and retire into their tower when bands of raiders were sighted.

The towers were designed so that they could not be easily demolished by the raiders. The lack of corners made them difficult to remove stones from the base. The only door to the towers were usually some feet above the ground and entrance was gained by the use of a ladder which was drawn up into the tower. Wooden floors separated various numbers of stories and a trapdoor provided access to the top. Each floor had one window in the form of an upright slot. Each slot faced in different directions so it was possible to observe the countryside and at the same time having only one or two windows at the most, visible from outside the tower. Thus the defenders could throw missiles from different directions and heights during a siege.

Food supplies and water stored in the tower for prolonged periods of isolation assured the defenders they could out-wait the raiders who seldom spent more than two or three days plundering. (In more recent times the water from Iona's tower well provided the only source of water for the island during a severe drought). In addition to a refuge from danger, round towers had many purposes. It was a belfry summoning the monks to assemble or pray. It was a landmark for those at sea approaching the island during a storm and a look-out station where pirates could be sighted bearing down on the island.

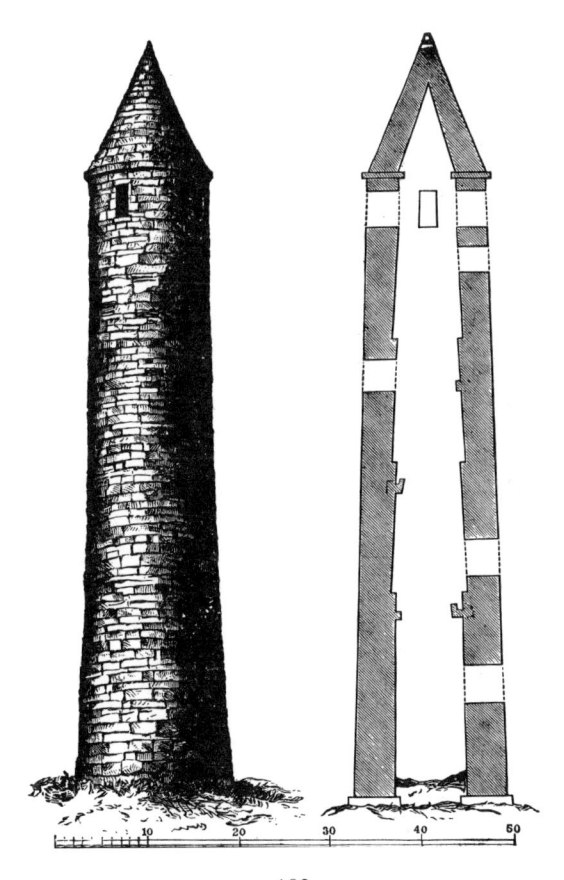

The only danger, for the monks using the tower for protection from raiders, was fire. In the event of the tower's timber flooring set alight by fire-tipped arrows, the strong draught caused by the tower's general design, (like a chimney) would give the occupants little chance of survival.

ABERNETHY ROUND TOWER
72 feet in height and 8 feet in basal diameter
lower part dated middle of 9th century A.D.

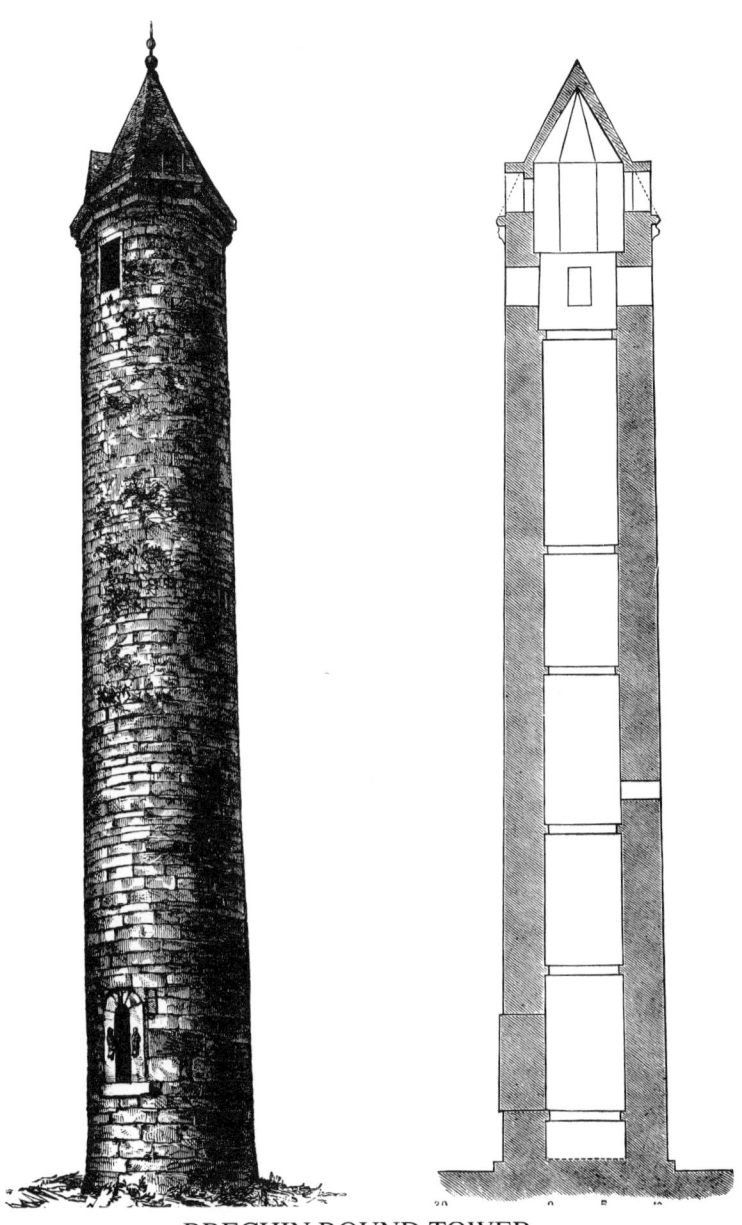

BRECHIN ROUND TOWER
86 feet 9 inches in height and 7 feet 11 inches
internal basal diameter. Typical Irish tower.

DOORWAY OF BRECHIN ROUND TOWER

Double peller-border on a raised band is also found on High Crosses and church doorways in Ireland. Over the doorway is a sculpture of the Crucifixion, a common representation in Ireland but rare in Pictland. At the foot of the doorway, outside the raised band, crouch two grotesque beasts. About 80 of these round towers still survive in Ireland, built during the Viking invasions – an example of "Heaven helps those who help themselves."

STREET OF THE DEAD

Immediately to the west of the Abbey was found the ancient stone road used as the Street of the Dead, for funeral trains bringing the bodies of men of renowned to be buried on Iona. It was found in 1962 when digging a trench. It was probably laid in the 12th century and was in a perfect state of preservation. The road went south past the cemetery, round the back of the Nunnery through a stone archway (now missing) to a small sandy beach called Martyr's Bay.

REILIG ORAN

Adjacent to the Abbey Church is the Graveyard of the Kings, known as Reilig Oran where Oran, the last of the ancient Druids was buried. Kenneth Mac Alpine, the first monarch of the United Kingdom of Picts and Scots, a kingdom whose foundation was laid by Columba, was also interred here in 860 A.D. This was the burial ground of the Scottish kings into the eleventh century. Beneath one of the royal grave slabs lies Duncan, the victim (according to Shakespeare) of Macbeth's infamous hospitality one stormy night in 1040. Macbeth lies near his victim.

In 1549, Donald Monro, later Archdeacon of the Isles said that in three tombs were buried 48 Scottish kings, 4 Irish Kings, and 8 Norwegian Kings. Six Kings of France are also reported to lie in the hallowed ground of St. Oran's Cemetery. Many of the great Highland chieftains are also buried in the Cemetery of the Kings. Among the illustrious names found here are the MacLeans, MacDonalds and the MacLeods.

These tombs for the most part have long since disappeared but stones gathered in a little chapel adjoining the cemetery represent Kings of Medieval periods. It is still the graveyard for the island and thus has been reverenced for over 1400 years.

In the ancient burying-ground of Reilig Oran is a small chapel 29 feet by 15 feet in dimensions and dedicated to St. Oran, a cousin of Columba. It is the oldest of the medieval ruins and is believed to have been built by Margaret, Queen of Scotland around 1074. Somerled, ruler of the Isles (cir 1164) or his son Reginald is reputed to have used it as a family mortuary chapel. The Doorway has a richly carved Norman arch of a later date than the chapel itself. The chapel was restored and re-roofed in 1957.

ST. ORAN'S CHAPEL

Grave-stones

FRONT AND END VIEW OF THE MONYMUSK RELIQUARY
AN EARLY CELTIC CASKET FOR HOLDING RELICS OF SCOTTISH CHURCH

THE CROSSES OF IONA

Few people realize that the Parent Crosses of the famed High Crosses of Ireland are located here on Iona, Scotland. Columba and his followers hammered out their faith as well as preached it. On the stone crosses, the Gospel was sculptured. In front of St. Columba's Chapel, traditionally held to be the site of the Shrine which housed the relics of the Saint, stands an exact replica made from a mold of St. John's Cross, the original having been blown down and broken in a gale in 1951. The cross originally had bosses, possibly of marble set into the stone. The original dates from the 10th century or earlier. The Celtic saints regarded St. John as their special patron.

Next to the Abbey well is the remnant of St. Matthew's Cross, one of the earliest. On the west side of the fragment remaining is a representation of the temptation of Adam and Eve carved upon it. The cross contains examples of interlaced work and serpents' heads. It is believed that the arms and head of this cross lie buried in the earth beside it.

A few feet away facing the door of the Abbey is the beautiful St. Martin's Cross from the 10th century. It is one of the most perfect examples of Celtic crosses in existence. It commemorates St. Martin, Patron Saint of France. The sculpture on its west side includes the Virgin and Child, Daniel in the lion's den, and David playing before Saul. The base contains a Gaelic inscription meaning, "Pray for the servant of Christ who made this cross."

The Celtic crosses are distinguished from all other crosses by its form which combines two symbols, the ring and the cross, the ring intersecting the arms and shaft of the cross. These Celtic crosses stand to tell the true story of Christ's sacrifice, for they have no figure of Christ nailed to them. They stand empty, for they represent a risen Christ. It is noteworthy that of the some two hundred fifty crosses of the early Celtic Church in Ireland no crucifixions are found.

South of the village along side the Street of the Dead is Maclean's Cross of the 15th century. It is believed to commemorate the Chief of the Malean Clan whose territory consisted mainly of Mull and its surrounding islands. Over 360 crosses are said to have been at one time existing on the Isle of Iona.

Maclean's Cross

FORM OF THE IRISH HIGH CROSS

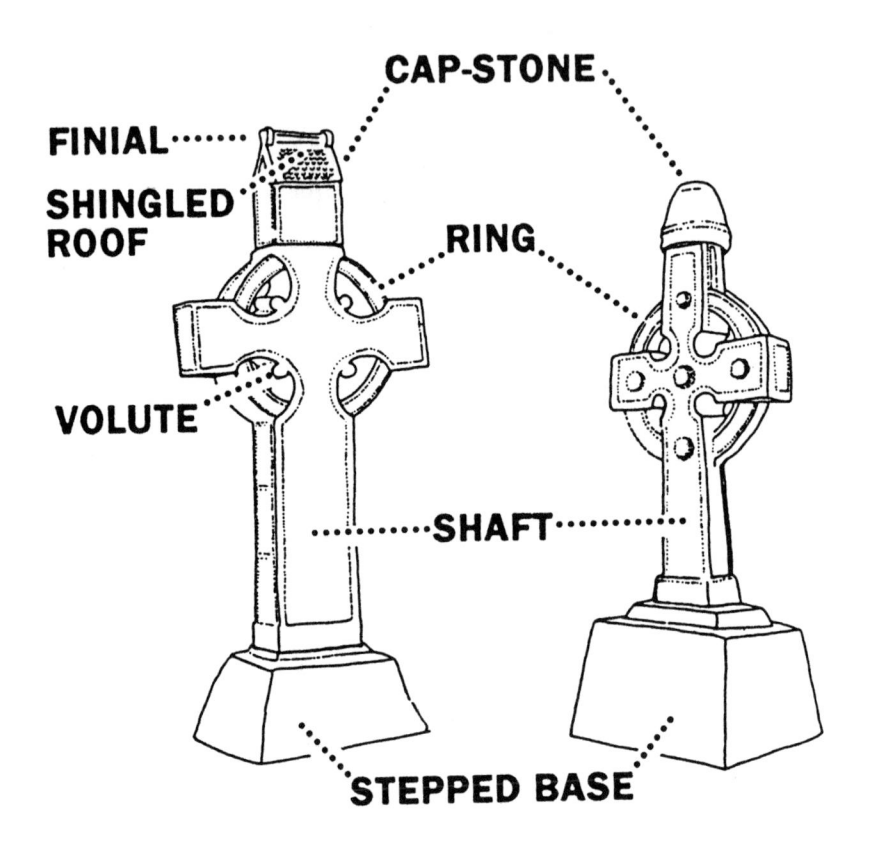

- FINIAL
- SHINGLED ROOF
- CAP-STONE
- RING
- VOLUTE
- SHAFT
- STEPPED BASE

In the earliest Christian art the Crucifixion was not depicted. The shame and ignominy associated with it made it for many years an unsuitable subject for portrayal. As a means of execution it remained in force until it was abolished by the Emperor Constantine. He became the champion of Christianity in the first part of the fourth century and is thought to have introduced the use of the Chi-Rho monogram, the first two letters of Christ's name in Greek. The shape of the Celtic Cross, in Christian iconography, symbolizes Christ in person.

In the early days of Christianity few people could read, and books were scarce. The Celtic monks, therefore, tried to teach using pictures and patterns. This is called symbolism. In those early days of Christianity the monks carved the crosses to illustrate a message. They chose certain things to stand for truths that they wanted to teach.

INTERLACED ORNAMENTS - A favorite way of decorating the crosses. The story they taught was that the cord that winds backwards and forwards stood for man's life wandering in and out of various places. It has no beginning and no ending, weaving in and out in its pilgrimage. Sometime there are two cords twisting over and under each other. One cord does not finish and the other begin, they intermingle all the time. The ancient teachers wanted to impress folks that man didn't have a life here quite alone and then suddenly die and begin another life in eternity, but that God sends His Eternal Spirit to help us in this life. The two are forever entwined.

Sometimes these intertwining cords are depicted as if they were knotted together. This was meant to suggest that in life there are many knotty problems to be unraveled. Sometimes they carved faces of demons in among the interlacing reminding the viewer of the pitfalls and temptations they will encounter in life. The vine spiral, so named to remind us of Christ's words, "I am the true vine."

THE STAG - This animal is carved to tell two stories. It was to teach the verse in Psalms "As the hart (stag) panteth after the water brooks, so panteth my soul after thee O God." The stag was like a picture of man's soul longing for God. The stag also taught another truth. In those far-off days the stag was hunted in the wild mountains of Scotland and came to be looked upon as the most hunted of all creatures. The stag was to represent an unhappy man being pursued by the hunter till he finds, in Christ alone, refuge and safety.

GROTESQUE ANIMALS - It is believed that the monks purposely made their carved animals (and birds) quaint and unlike the real thing in keeping with the second commandment. "Thou shalt not make unto thee any graven image." Often, for instance, they mixed the animal (or bird) into a lovely pattern of leaves and flowers.

DOGS - Dogs are sometimes used in the carvings to denote faithfulness. A bird stands for friendship. Fish were often used in the carvings because they were symbols of all knowledge, and as they swim throughout the seas of the world, they represent the spread of Christianity. Later they were used as a secret symbol to denote the homes where the Christian disciples lived.

ROUNDS OR BOSSES - These represent the sun and are often associated with serpents. Long before Christ was born, men used to worship the sun for its light and warmth. Sometimes the sun was darkened, even in the middle of the day. Of course this would have been an eclipse of the sun. The early sunworshipers knew nothing about the meaning of eclipses and believed when the sun "went out" that it had been vanquished in a battle with the serpent of evil who was always sneaking about in the sky. When the sun shone out after "the battle" they supposed the serpent had been defeated after all.

After centuries of accepting this explanation, their wise men decided the sun always won the battle each time, and the serpent was always punctual. They could know exactly when he was coming to try to set up the sun. In time they worked out a calendar of time based on the "eclipses". In some ways it was a better calendar than ours today. They did not have to move in an extra day each year and had no need for leap years.

As time went on the more certain they became that the serpent would appear at exactly the right second. The ancient Druids began to think of the serpent as not evil but as punctual, always appearing at the right time and never failing. Finally the serpent became the symbol of Eternity. The "everlasting pattern" that we associate with the Celts is serpent-like in its spirals or coils. St. Martin's Cross shows how beautifully the old idea was carried on into Christianity.

BIBLE SCENES - Certain Bible stories are found on the ancient Celtic Crosses. Adam and Eve tells the story of man's first sin and his need for saving. Usually they are shown standing on each side of a tree. The Virgin Mary with the Child Jesus reminds people that because they needed a Savior, God sent Jesus, His only Son as a babe. There is a picture of this on the west side of St. Martin's Cross. Daniel in the Lion's Den is found on many crosses.

THE GALLEY OR NORSE SHIP - When the Hebrides were under the power of Norway, many Norwegians came over and settled, and, of course, the two races married one with the other and copied each other's ways and customs. The Norwegians were famous seafarers and their ships became well known. Pictures of these ships began to appear on the coats-of-arms, and it is these Norse galleys that appear so often on Hebridean grave-stones. Each branch of the clans chose slightly different ships or different rigging, in order to show which family they belonged to. For instance, the Argyll branch of the Campbells have three sweeps (as the oars are called), and the Inverneil Campbells have five sweeps. But as well as being coats-of-arms and family crests the ship-pictures were also used to tell stories, like the other symbols. The ships with sails set represented man passing through the storms and tempests of life, and if the ship's sails were furled (that is looped, and lashed to the cross-bar) it meant that the ship had reached safe harbour. A man had finished the voyage of life and was safe with God. So it became a favorite picture for a gravestone.

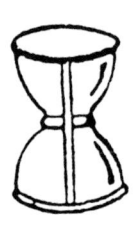

THE HOUR GLASS - This symbol reminded folk of the swift flight of time and the brief life of man on earth.

PLACES FOR EXPLORATION

Except for the buildings, the Island of Iona has changed little from what Columba gazed upon some thirteen hundred years ago. Following are a few places for exploring. Perhaps visitors will discover other places of interest.

MARTYR'S BAY

The first of the Viking attacks on Iona took place in A.D. 795 when extensive damage was done to the monatic buildings. Seven years later the Abbey was gutted by the Danes (Norsemen) and in 806 the event was repeated yet more savagely. This time they killed sixty-eight monks on the beach close to the present jetty. The beach is now known as Martyr's Bay. After this raid most of the monks moved to Kells in Ireland, taking with them the gold and silver shrine of St. Columba containing the remains of the Saint. A few monks remained on Iona to guard the remaining treasure.

Unwisely, perhaps, the succeeding Abbot brought back the shrine and the treasure to Iona from Ireland.

WHITE STRAND OF THE MONKS

On the northeast side of the island is the White Strand of the Monks (Traigh Bhan Manach). Eighty years after the raid and slaughter at Martyr's Bay marauding Danes in 986 paid another visit to Iona. The pirates burst into the church one dark winter morning during the celebration of Mass and killed Blathmac, the acting superior, together with fifteen monks. The monks had been warned the Danes were coming and had time to bury their treasures including the richly ornamented shrine of Columba's relics, but failed to reach the protection within the tower.

Blathmac had asked to be kept in ignorance as to where the treasures were hid, in the event he might be tortured and reveal their hiding place. When the Danes commanded Blathmac to hand over the treasures he was of course unable to do so, and he and his monks were all taken to this little bay and killed on its white sands as they stood with back to the jagged rocks at the north end of the bay.

There were two reasons for these raids. The pirates knew that the monasteries contained rich treasures and would be defended only by lightly armed monks and thus would be easy to plunder. Also, on the Continent at that time, Charlemagne, in the name of Christianity, was slaughtering the heathen tribes of north Germany, near Denmark. The Danes naturally hated the Church, who they held responsible for the killing of their pagan kinsmen.

ANGEL'S HILL (OR FAIRY MOUND)

Angel's Hill (in Gaelic Cnoc nan Aingeal) or Great Fairy-Mound (in Gaelic Sithean Mor) is a grassy knoll just south of the extremity of the road leading to the Machair. It is one of the "fairy knolls" of Iona of pre-Christian times. Folklore says the "Wee Folk were wont to hold revel in these knolls and mortals passing by have heard faint strains of fairy music proceeding from within."

In later days, the Angel's Hill was the scene of a general cavalcade at the Feast of St. Michael, the natives coursing round the hillock on horseback – a ceremony common throughout the Western Isles. Trenholme, in his story of Iona says, "Michael of the Snow-white Steeds appears with Mary and Columkill in the old songs and hymns of the Islesmen, as a great protector by sea and shore."

PORT LARAICHEAN (BAY OF RUINS)

Port Laraichean lies just west of Columba's Bay. A little back from the beach, on a grassy terrace of artificial construction, are the foundations of six or seven circular stone huts, with a larger and squarer one on a rock near by. These are believed to be the oldest buildings on the island. Sheltered all around by high rocks, save where it looks out on to the sea, "the hamlet could be well defended with bows and arrows."

SPOUTING CAVE

On the west shore is rocky cavern known as the Spouting Cave. At certain tides and winds, tons of sea-water are forced up to a great height with a loud roaring noise through an opening in its roof. It was on this side of the island that the village originally stood, near the fields which produced the islander's crops and food. It was not until the last century that with their increasing dependence upon stores and food from the mainland, they began to build their homes near the landing place until the present village (Baile Mor) came into being.

IONA Marble Quarry
How to get there

••••••• Direct Route
ooooooo Alternative Route

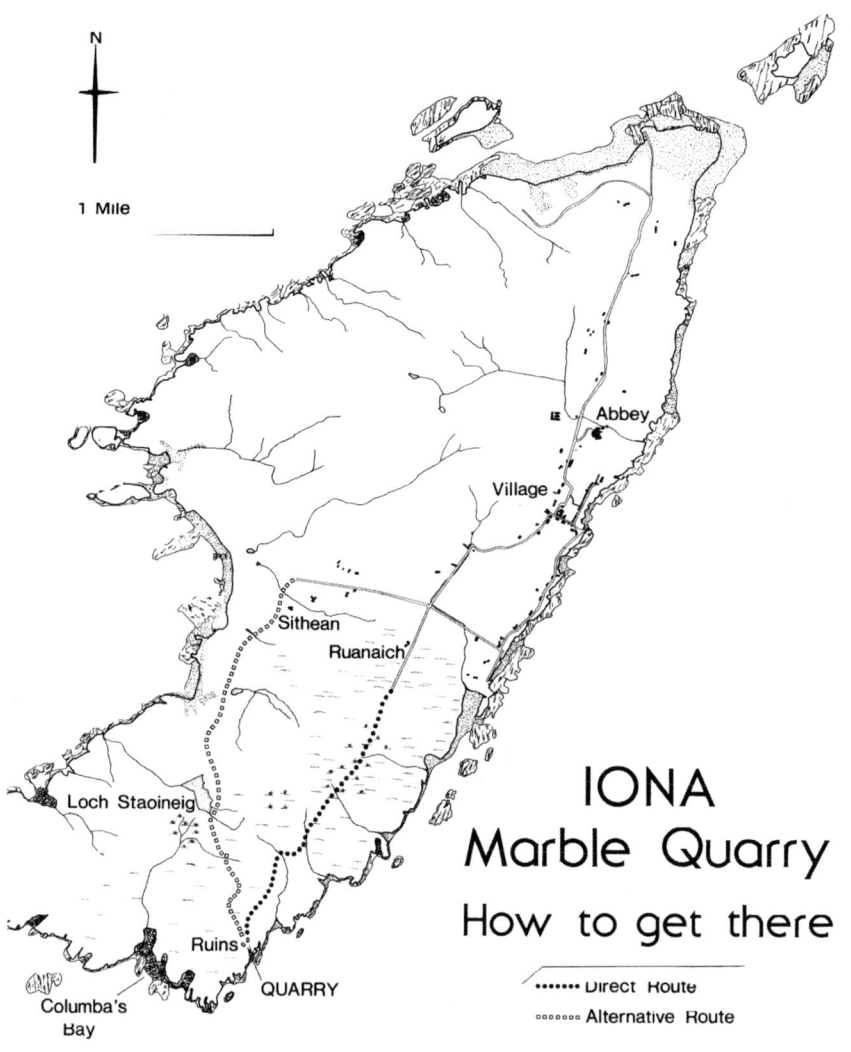

The more direct route via Ruanaich involves some upland walking across featureless moorland; keep to the higher ground and avoid descending too early to the other coves along the south-eastern coast. The longer route via the Machair beyond Sithean follows the track to the reservoir at Loch Staoineg; thence take to higher ground descending directly to the quarry keeping the paths down to Columba Bay on the right. Look for the ruined huts below which the quarry will come into view.

IONA MARBLE QUARRY

The rock formation on much of Iona dates from the pre-Cambrian period, probably 1500 million years old, which are some of the earliest known rock formations in Britain. Although metamorphosed igneous rock preponderate, there are areas of metamorphosed sedimentary rocks on the northwest coast consisting of a band of marble about 7 feet wide. It is a pinkish-grey color mottled with green serpentine, known as the "silver-stone."

The Marble Quarry of Iona lies at the foot of a ravine, facing the Sound, and not far from the south-western extremity of the Island. Its position, shut in as it is by cliff and rocks, makes it difficult to visit. Access by land involves an arduous journey over a mile on the marshy and treacherous upland of the southern part of Iona before reaching the eastern side of the island. Then it is a steep climb down to the quarry itself. The approach by sea is hazardous due to the fact that the rocky beach is totally exposed to the south and seldom is there a calm day for embarking or disembarking by boat.

The main occurrence of marble is at the site of the "Quarry," on the shoreline about 500 yards northeast of the most southerly point of the island. The rock is a forsterite tremolite marble, mainly white in color and owing its peculiar beauty to streaks and patches of light-green serpentine. The marble forms a nearly vertical band 20 to 40 feet thick running somewhat east of north. It has been quarried for up to 100 yards inland from the shore before it disappears under a massive overburden of rocks. It has been suggested that the Iona pebbles of marble and serpentine which are thrown up on the beaches of the south coast of the island, particularly in St. Columba's Bay, are derived from a submarine extension of the marble in that area.

The marble was quarried extensively from medieval times, working to particular or individual demands. By 1819 most of the marble bed had been removed leaving only the sides of the quarry and those parts which were inaccessible to the quarrymen by reason of the sea. About 1907 the quarry was restarted and by the outbreak of World War I was again abandoned. Machinery for lifting and cutting the marble and a rusty gas engine can still be seen in the quarry. Most of the marble had to be removed from the quarry by way of the sea.

Records indicate the quarry was worked intermittently from at least medieval times onward, seemingly working to particular and often individual demands. Between 1907-1914, machinery was installed in order to cut the marble more easily into slabs for transportation. Today, marble is only rarely quarried and then for specific use. An example is the altar of the Iona Abbey and occasionally a grave headstone. A souvenir industry has grown up based on the island's marble, but outside of Iona much of the "Iona marble" offered for sale today originated elsewhere and mined in Connemara.

MACHINERY FOR LIFTING AND CUTTING MARBLE

FLOWERS OF IONA

The flora of Iona is interestingly different from that of Mull and the other neighboring islands. In addition to mosses and ferns, there are over two hundred plants that have recognizable "flowers," that grow plentifully on the roadsides and on the arable land. Many of these plants have been introduced in the course of the intensive agriculture of the island.

The hill area of Iona is heavily grazed, and the soil is acid and comparatively infertile. Two main types of vegetation are found in this area: the heath plants, and the bog plants which grow in the drier parts. The North End of the island behind the dunes has very similar vegetation to the machair, or grassland, but because of its proximity to the sandy shore, is less stable. Sand is sometimes blown over the grass, and some areas are laid bare by the wind.

There are five distinct habitants on Iona which are illustrated on the following pages:

Sea Holly

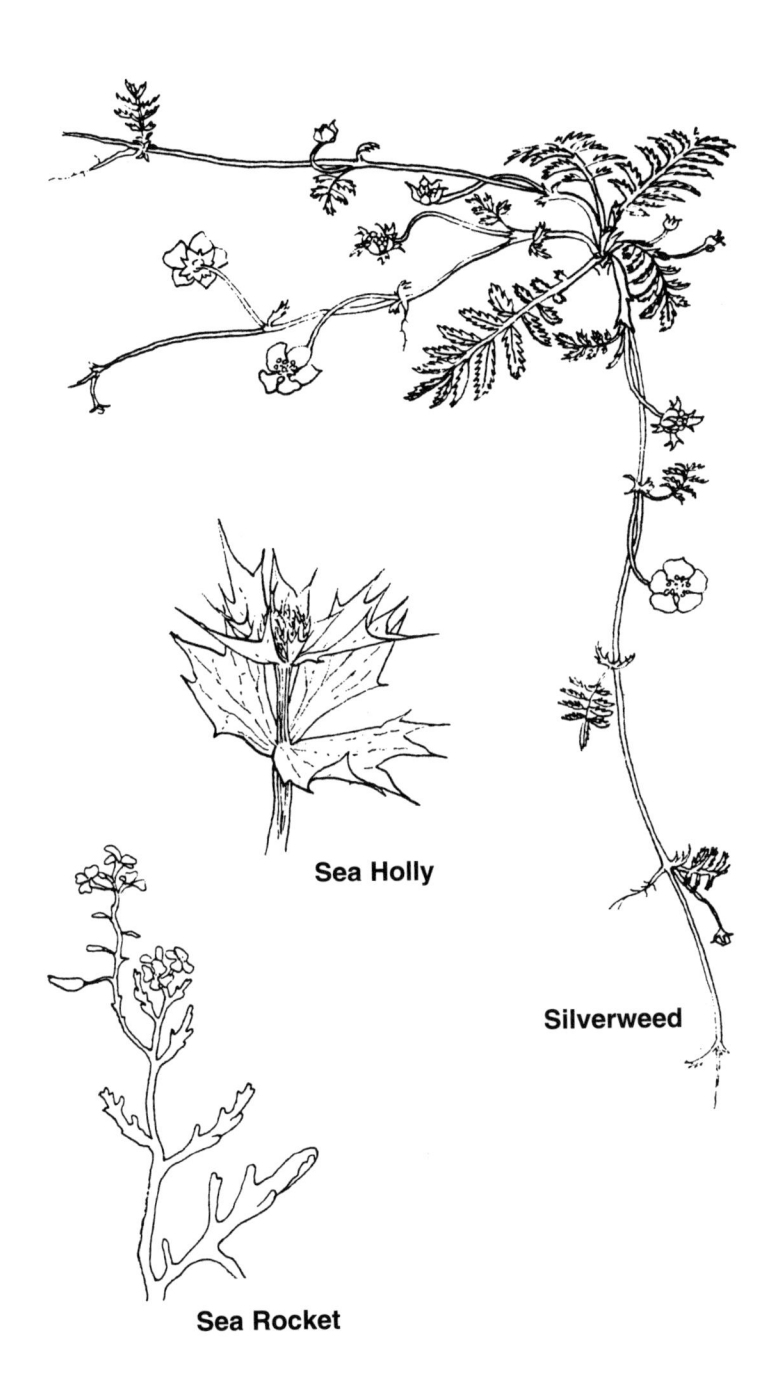

Silverweed

Sea Rocket

SANDY SHORE

Land plants growing on the sandy shore must overcome many problems: the sand moves, the winds are strong and salty, sunlight is reflected fiercely from the sand, and there is a shortage of fresh water and humus. Yet the beaches of Iona are colonized above high water with great persistence by a variety of land plants. One of the most striking and common of these is Silverweed. The name refers to the silvery leaves, and the silky hairs which give this silver appearance. The hairs protect the leaves from the fierce sun and prevent too much water-loss. Silverweed rapidly colonises the shore by sending out long, red, creeping stems which can root at the nodes (like the strawberry plant, which belongs to the same family).

Sea Rocket is anchored in the sand by a very long slender root, which can draw water from deep below the surface. This water can then be stored in the very fleshy leaves. The fruits of Sea Rocket can float. The seeds are unaffected by sea water, so the plants are distributed along the coast in this way – like coconuts in the Pacific Islands. At one time some seed must have been blown onto the shore of Storm Island, for a large colony of Sea Rocket edges the beach there.

Sea Holly has sharply spined leaves which protect the plant from grazing animals, and a thick waxy coating which prevents too much water-loss. Sea Holly was recorded in Iona in the Second Statistical Account (1845), and, having died out, was re-introduced in 1950; it is just now becoming established. The candied root was once used as an aphrodisiac. Its efficacy, however, is uncertain, and its rarity should prohibit such a use. Where it is common it performs the important function of binding the sand and preventing the shore from encroaching on the land. In Iona this function is carried out by Sea Marram Grass, which forms the North End and other dunes. Marram does not withstand salt and therefore is found only well above high water. The stiff leaves of Marram trap the blown sand. As the level of the sand rises up the stem, new roots are formed, and new leaves arise. Eventually there is an enormous network of stems and roots holding the sand. The leaves are often curled over the central rib in dry windy weather for conservation of water. After the Marram Grass has become established in one area, other plants begin to grow amongst it. Eventually a meadow will take over and the Marram will die out.

Storksbill

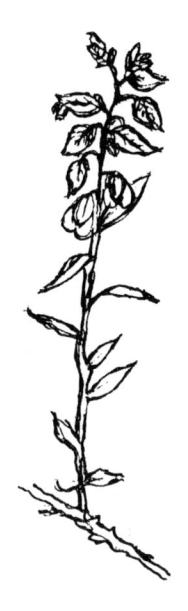

Milkwort

Wild Carrot

Birdsfoot Trefoil

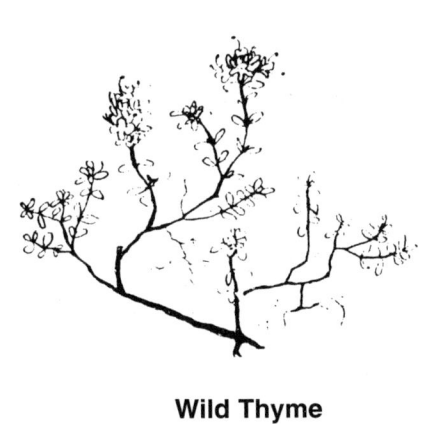

Wild Thyme

MACHAIR

Level grassland called machair is found on the West coast of many of the Inner and Outer Hebrides and is often used, as in Iona, as common grazing. At first sight the vegetation would seem to consist only of smooth closely-cropped grass, but on closer examination many small flowering plants are discovered. These are often small specimens of plants which grow much larger in more sheltered, less grazed parts of the island. The plants illustrated here are half life-size, and it is especially interesting to note the height of the Wild Carrot. Normally the stem of the inflorescence is one to one-and-a-half feet, whilst on the machair the inflorescence is almost on the ground. Seen growing in this way, the plant illustrates better the American common name Queen Anne's Lace than our prosaic "Carrot." The foliage of many of the plants grows along the ground amongst the grass, and the leaves are either small, as in Thyme, or much divided, as in Storksbill.

Two of the plants illustrated take their names from the shape of the fruits. The Birdsfoot-trefoil fruit has very long pods, and when three or four develop on one head they together look like the foot of a bird. It is the individual fruits of the Storksbill which have the appearance of the head of a stork, the long bill being the remains of the style. When the fruit is ripe, the style will split into five from the base outwards, and curl up, one seed going with each part of the style as it shoots away from the parent plant.

Thyme covers large areas of the machair, and in July turns whole banks purple. The scent of the leaves is less strong than Garden Thyme, but can be smelt when the leaves are crushed.

The flowers of Milkwort are usually purplish blue, but can be pink or white. The colour is in the two larger inner sepals, which enclose the rest of the flower. As the fruit develops, these sepals turn green.

The machair was once cultivated, and the ridges can be clearly seen running east-west. These would have been formed by seaweed brought up from the shore in autumn and winter and laid in strips, gradually building up a rich soil suitable for the cultivation of cereals or potatoes.

Scottish Heather

Bell Heather

Cross-leaved Heath

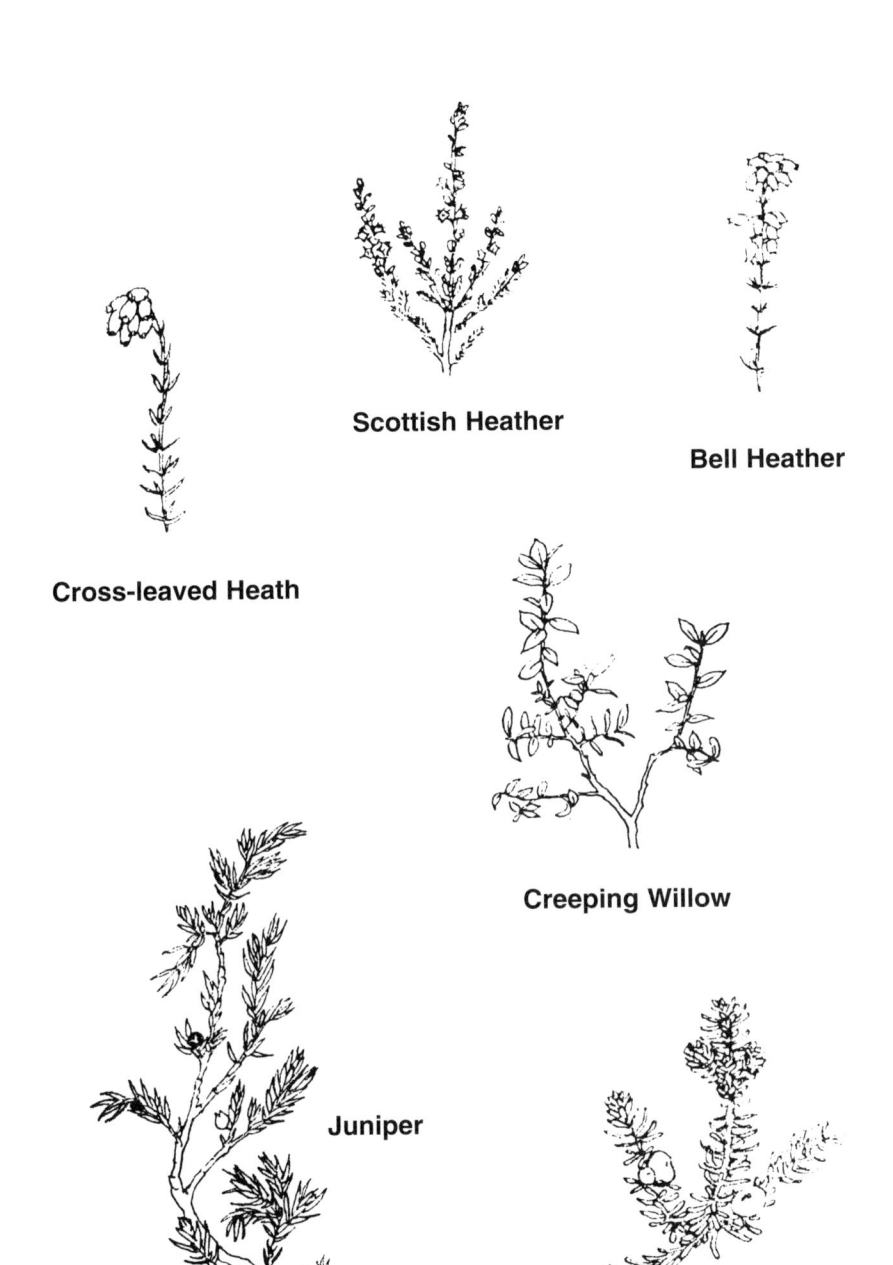

Creeping Willow

Juniper

Crowberry

HEATH PLANTS

Many heath plants are low, evergreen shrubs, their small leaves being adapted in different ways to withstand exposure to the wind. Scottish Heather is plentiful in Iona, flowering in September, which distinguishes it from Cross-leaved Heath and Bell Heather, which both flower in July and August. The delicate, pale pink flowers of the Cross-leaved Heath are the largest of the three, and the name describes the leaf arrangement. The flowers of Bell Heather are bright purplish-pink, turning dull purple as they die.

Juniper is found mainly in the South End of the island. It suffers from the practice of heather burning, and in areas recently burned the dead silver-grey Juniper branches can often be seen amongst the renewed heather shoots. The amazing contortions of these branches can be traced along the ground, showing how this native tree of Scotland adapts itself to a wind-swept habitat. It grows vigorously in areas which have escaped the heather fires, sometimes bearing the bitter, bloomed-black fruits, which were once used to flavour gin. The seedlings are often destroyed by grazing, but once plants are established, grazing will not kill them.

The Crowberry is an undistinguished plant common on the drier parts of the hill. The male and female flowers grow on separate plants, appearing in March and April. The pollen is carried by wind from the long purple anthers of the male to the short sticky stigmas of the female. It is rare to find the ripe black fruits except on rocky islets or headlands which are inaccessible to sheep.

Also common, especially on higher ground, is the Creeping Willow. Like the Crowberry, the male and female flowers are on separate plants, but the pollen is carried by insects attracted to the nectar in the female catkins. In May the fruits, which are any colour from orange-red to green, burst open, releasing the seeds, each with its parachute of long, white, silky hairs. In summer many of the Creeping Willow leaves have prominent orange-red galls. If these are cut open, a grub will be seen inside.

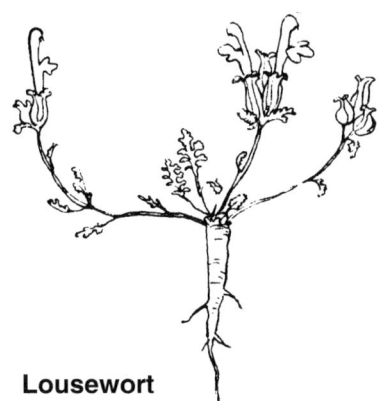

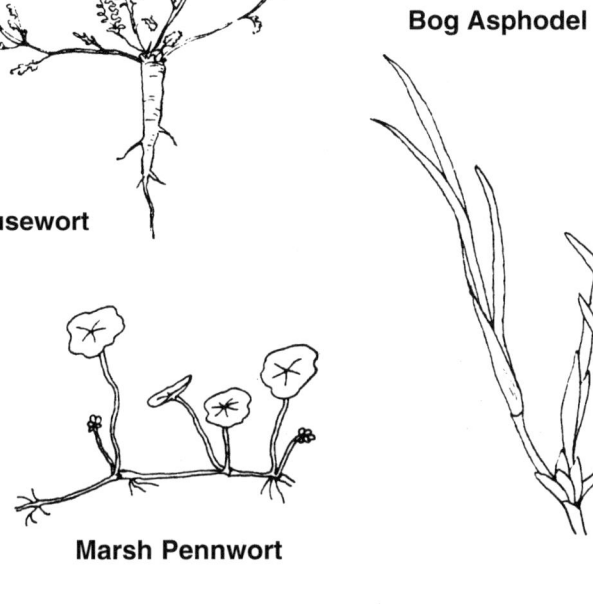

Lousewort

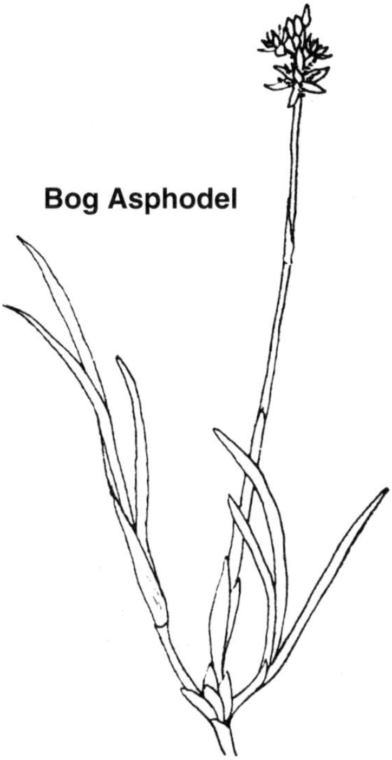

Bog Asphodel

Marsh Pennwort

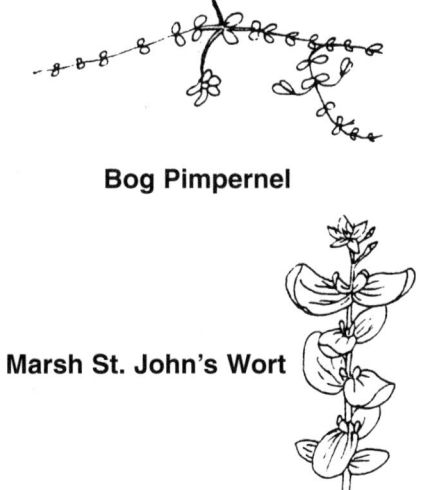

Sundew

Bog Pimpernel

Marsh St. John's Wort

BOG PLANTS

Bog plants are very different in appearance from heath plants, most being perennials, the aerial parts dying back completely in the autumn. The following spring the plant will grow again to produce large or tender leaves, and brightly coloured flowers.

The roots of bog plants are submerged much of the year in stagnant water, and to ensure oxygen supply to the root tissues many have special air channels in their roots. Because the soil is acid, wet and lacking in oxygen, there are few bacteria to release nitrogen from the breakdown of dead plant material. Bog plants have various methods of obtaining this necessary element, one of the strangest being that of the insectiverous plants. In Iona there are two types. Sundew has a rosette of round leaves, and each leaf covered with hairs having globular sticky tips. If an insect falls on the leaf is the hairs curl round and trap it. The more it struggles, the more the hairs close round until it dies. The plant secretes juices which dissolve the soft parts of the insect, and these are absorbed into the plant. The Butterworts have larger leaves then Sundew, and instead of hairs have yellow glands producing a sticky substance which will trap small insects. Iona has two species of Butterwort: Common Butterwort flowering in May-June, and Pale Butterwort flowering in July-August. The latter has smaller and paler flowers.

Some bog plants obtain nutrients lacking in the soil by having fungi associated with their roots. The fungi is able to break down raw humus. This is the method used by the orchids. The Early Purple Orchid and the Heath Spotted Orchid are two of the most striking plants of the island bogs. Lousewort, and its near relation Red Rattle obtain extra nutrients by being semi-parasites, sucking food from the roots of neighbouring grasses. Their leaves are small and red.

Marsh St. John's Wort is unlike any of the other St. John's Worts. The leaves are covered with white hairs which trap air enabling the plant to float when the water level is high.

One of the smallest bog plants is Bog Pimpernel, which is common but often goes unnoticed as the pale pink flowers shut in dull weather.

Lovage

English Stonecrop

Rose-root

Thrift

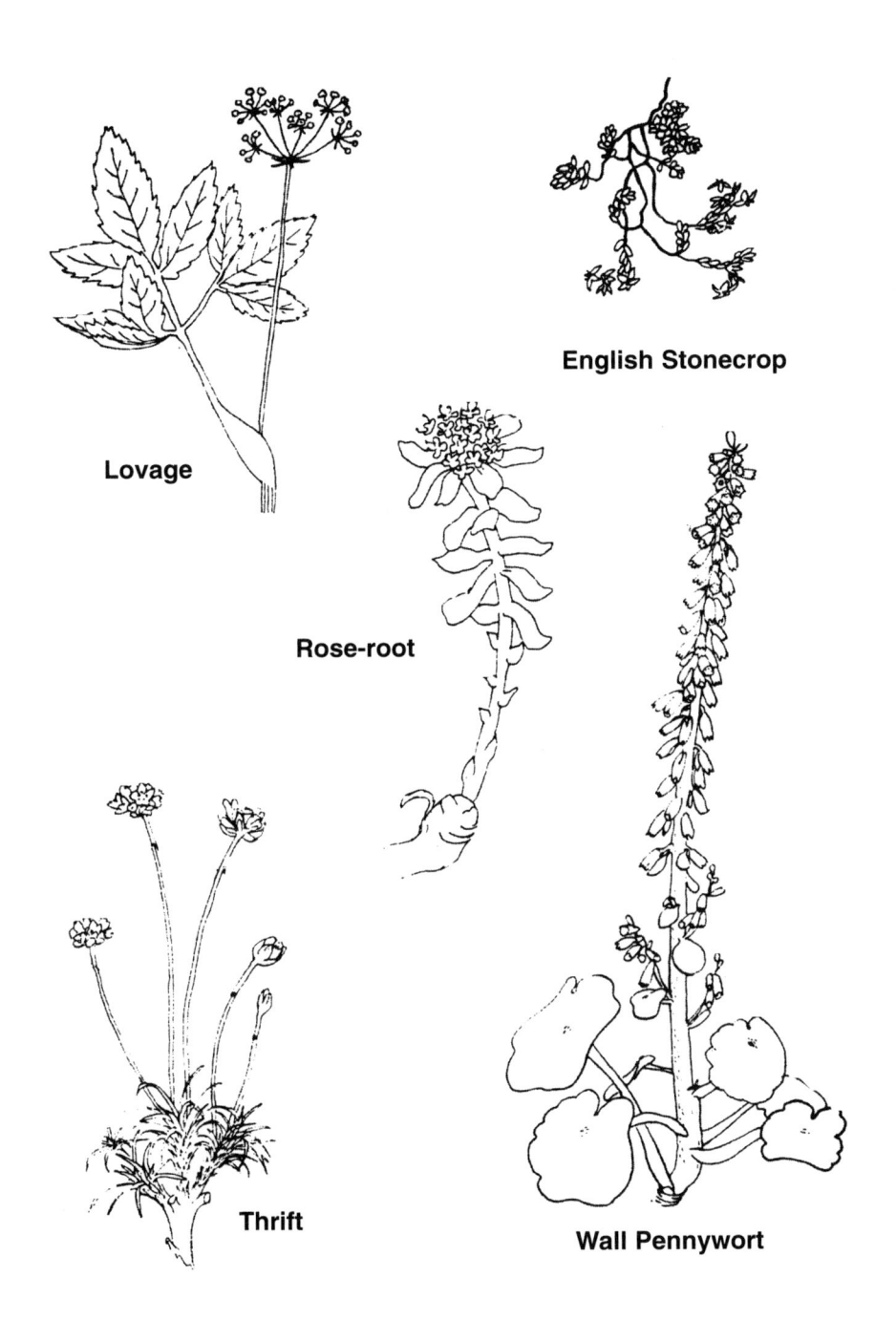

Wall Pennywort

ROCK FACE

Some flowers grow on what seems to be bare rock. However, rocks are rarely completely bare botanically, unless they have recently been split open. Lichens and mosses cover the rock faces. They gradually eat into the surface, and where there are cracks soil is built up from the crumbled rock and decayed vegetable matter. If seeds of flowering plants land in these cracks, they may germinate, but only plants specially adapted to this habitat will survive.

English Stonecrop exists here because its leaves are extremely fleshy and can store water. The other plants illustrated all have very strong root systems which grow deep into the rock crevices, crumbling and splitting the rock and creating more soil. Thrift, as well as being able to grow in rock, is also adapted to withstand salty conditions and will be found growing far down the rocky shore. Wall Pennywort has a curious appearance with its spikes of greenish yellow flowers rising above the radical leaves. The other name of this plant, Navelwort, comes from the appearance of these leaves which have a depression in the center where the leaf-stalk joins the leaves. This leaf is similar to that of Marsh Pennywort, but the two plants are not related.

Rose-Root has male and female flowers on separate plants, the illustration showing the male. Both flower in May or June, and in July the orange-red fruits of the female might be mistaken for the flower. The leaves are very succulent, like those of English Stonecrop, and are blue-green tinged with red. The name comes from the fact that the dying root is said to smell of roses.

The leaves of Lovage are bright green and leathery, distinguishing this plant from the many other members of the Umbellifer family found in Iona. The stems are tinged with purple. When the leaves are crushed, they have a delicious smell and have been used as a pot herb.

One of the interesting plants of the rock habitat in Iona is Valerian, which flourishes on the Nunnery walls. This is not indigenous but has spread from one packet of seeds sown forty years ago.

THE WHITE PACK-HORSE BIDS FAREWELL TO THE DYING SAINT COLUMBA

"*Ecce albus occurrit caballus, obediens servitor, qui scilicet lactaria bocetum inter et monasterium vascula gestare consuerverat. Hic ad Sanctum accedens, mirum dictu, captu in sinu eius ponens, ut credo inspirante Deo, cui omne animal rerum sapit sensu quo iusserit ipse Creator, dominum a se suum mox emigraturum, et ipsum ultra non visurum sciens, coepit plangere, ubertimque, quasi homo, lacrymas in gremium Sancti fundere, et valde spumans flere.*"

PROPHECY OF ST. COLUMBA

The prophecies of St. Columba are controversial. The opinion of the Irish scholars range from outright forgeries to authentic and genuine. However, the fact is that they have for centuries been an integral part of Irish life and folklore. One of the most important poems is a translation from the hand of Adamnan and claimed by Nicholas O'Kearney (1855), the Irish historian, to have originated from the hand of St. Columba himself. Several translations have been published. The most popular one is as follows:

Addressed to St. Brendan

The time shall come O Brendan,
When you would feel it painful to reside in Erin;
The sons of kings shall be few in number,
And the literati shall be deprived of dignity.

They (the people) will continue to reside in stone mansions,
They will inhabit the islets on the lakes;
They will not perform charitable acts.
And truth shall not remain in them.

They will plunder the property of the church,
They will take preys of cattle furtively;
They will treat men of learning disrespectfully,
Afterwards they themselves shall become powerless.

The sons of kings (great men) will become archaeologists,
The descendants of sages shall become ignorant;
They will be continually sneering at each other,
They will employ themselves at reading and writing.

They will scoff at acts of humanity,
And at irreproachable humility;
Men of learning shall become rare among them,
And ignorant men shall prosper.

There shall come times of dark affliction,
Of scarcity, of sorrow, and of wailing;
In the latter ages of the world's existence,
And monarchs will be addicted to falsehood.

Neither justice nor covenant will be observed,
By any one people of the race of Adam;
They will become hard-hearted and penurious,
And will be devoid of piety.

Men will become murmurers, –
The trees shall not bear the usual quantity of fruit;
Fisheries shall become unproductive,
And the earth shall not yield its usual abundance.

The clergy will become fosterers,
In consequence of the tidings of wretchedness,
Churches shall be held in bondage, (private property),
By the all-powerful men of the day.

Inclement weather, and famine shall come,
Hatred, malignity, and despair,
The natural span of human life shall be abridged.
And fishes will forsake the rivers.

The people oppressed by want of food, shall pine to death,
Meanwhile they shall be bound in slavery;
And in consequence of their enmity to one another,
Dreadful storms and hurricanes shall afflict them.

Judges will administer injustice,
Under the sanction of powerful, outrageous kings;
The common people will adopt false principles,
Oh, how lamentable shall be their position!

Doctors of science shall have cause to murmur,
They will become niggardly in spirit;
The aged will mourn in deep sorrow,
On account of the woeful times that shall prevail.

Cemeteries shall become all red (dug up),
In consequence of the wrath that will follow sinners;
Wars and contentions shall rage,
In the bosom of every family.

Kings (great men) shall be steeped in poverty,
They will become inhospitable to their guests;
The voice of the parasite will be more agreeable to them
Than the melody of the harp touched by the sages' finger.

Their candles shall be quenched,
Without intermission each sabbath day;
In consequence of the general prevalence of sinful practices,
Humility shall produce no fruit.

The professors of science shall not be rewarded,
Amiability shall not characterize the people;
Prosperity and hospitality shall not exist,
But niggardliness and destitution will assume their place.

The changes of seasons shall produce only half their verdure,
The regular festivals of the church will not be observed;
All classes of men shall be filled
With hatred and enmity towards each other.

The people will not associate affectionately with each other,
During the great festivals of the seasons;
They will live devoid of justice and rectitude,
Up from the youth of tender age to the aged.

The clergy shall be led into error,
By the misinterpretation of their reading;
The relics of the saints will be considered powerless,
Every race of mankind will become wicked!

They will construct islands,
Upon the pools of clear water (lakes);
Numberless diseases shall then prevail,
When Athe-na-cuilte shall be drained.

Sons of kings will not have sureties of kine.
Fortifications will be built narrow;
During those times of dreadful danger,
Persons born to inheritances shall be sorrowful.

Young women will become unblushing,
And aged people will be of irascible temper;
The kine will seldom be productive, as of old;
Lords will become murderers.

Young people will decline in vigour,
They will despise those who shall have hoary hair;
There shall be no standard by which morals may be regulated,
And marriages will be solemnized without witnesses.

Troublous shall be the latter ages of the world,
According to the Book of Truth: –
The clergy shall become ignorant,
Concerning the real festivities of the church.

The dispositions of the generality of men I will point out,
From the time they shall abandon hospitable habits –
With the view of winning honour for themselves,
They will hold each other as objects for ridicule.

I am Columbkille,
A prophet that speaks with perspicuity;
I can discern in my little book,
The clear explanation of all knowledge.

The possessors of abundance shall fall,
Through the multiplicity of their falsehoods;
Covetousness shall take possession of every glutton,
And when satiated their arrogance will know no bounds.

Between the mother and daughter,
Anger and bitter sarcasms shall continuously exist;
Neighbours will become treacherous,
Cold, and false-hearted towards each other.

The gentry will become grudgeful,
With respect to their trifling donations;
And blood relations will become cool towards each other,
Church livings shall become lay property.

All classes of people will be addicted to robbery,
Lords will become cold blooded murderers;
Ill-will and exclusive dealings,
Shall subsist between father and son.

Such is the description of the people,
Who shall live in the ages to come;
More unjust and iniquitous shall be
Every succeeding race of men!

                              The time shall come, &c.

CELTIC SONGS AND POEMS

One of the supreme achievements of the Celtic Church was to give birth to the wonderful "corpus" of English poetry. Also many beautiful Gaelic songs that are still sung in Scotland can undoubtedly be traced back to the poetic and musical tradition which the Church inaugurated. Many of these Celtic prayers and poems show the intense awareness of God's presence in the lives of the simple farming and fishing people of the Hebrides. Their sense of God's immediacy in daily living is precisely what so many people are urgently searching for today.

Contrary to popular belief that Celtic poetry is something typically mystical or vaguely pantheistic, the Gaelic people found it entirely natural to see God in every movement and at every level of their ordinary lives. In their conversations and songs they addressed "the great God of life, the Father of all living," in words which were at once homely and eloquent – presenting to Him their needs and desires, fully and familiarly, and yet also with awe and deference. Their prayers were songs, most of them designed to be sung privately, intoned softly or crooned secretly. However, certain of their songs or prayers were used in communal gatherings and rituals.

The material things of daily life almost inevitably became a way to God for a people who always speak of soul and body with equal respect. They perceived a world in which the division of sacred and secular seemed irrelevant. The Gaelic people found God lovingly concerned with all aspects of their lives and felt themselves walking not only in His presence but close to the saints and angels too. Almost as a matter of course they assumed that they were surrounded by a multitude of spiritual beings, near throughout the day and nearer still in the hours of sleep. The involvement of the saints was taken for granted and forms a constant subject in a greater number of their poems.

> "The holy apostles guarding,
> The gentle martyr's guarding,
> The nine angels' guarding,
> Be cherishing, be aiding me.
> The God of the elements guarding,
> The loving Christ's guarding,
> The Holy Spirit's guarding.
> Be cherishing, be aiding me."

An amazing vision of the universe is perceived in the Gaelic poems dealing with God's creation. The sun, moon, animals, and crops are felt to have the need to receive a blessing. Sunrise each day brought a prayer of thanks to the great God of life for the glory of the sun and for the goodness of its light to the children of man and to the animals of the world. Then when the sun set in the western horizon a prayer would be intoned:

> "I am in hope, in its proper time
> That the great and gracious God
> Will not put out for me the light of grace
> Even as thou doest leave me this night."

And at the sight of the new moon:

> "He who created thee
> Created me likewise:
> He who gave thee weight and light
> Gave to me life and death."

The Gaelic (Celts) recognized that everything good comes from God and is to be enjoyed; one is enslaved if they care for anything in ways that exclude the Giver:

> "It were as easy for Jesu
> To renew the withered tree
> As to wither the new
> Were it His will to do so.
>   Jesu! Jesu! Jesu!
>   Jesu! met is were to praise Him.
>
> There is no plant in the ground,
> But it is full of His virtue,
> There is no form in the strand
> But it is full of His blessing.
>   Jesu! Jesu! Jesu!
>   Jesu! met is were to praise Him.
>
> There is no life in the sea,
> There is no creature in the river,
> There is naught in the firmament
> But proclaims His goodness.

> Jesu! Jesu! Jesu!
> Jesu! met is were to praise Him.
>
> There is no bird on the wing,
> There is no star in the sky,
> There is nothing beneath the sun
> But proclaims His goodness.
> Jesu! Jesu! Jesu!
> Jesu! met is were to praise Him."

As the men set out for their day's work, leaving home to fish or farm, they would say a short prayer, singing or intoning it sometimes in an almost inaudible undertone. They could assume the companionship of God with such confidence that they were actually laughing as they went.

> My walk this day with God
> My walk this day with Christ
> My walk this day with Spirit
> The Threefold all-kindly
> Ho! ho! ho! the Threefold all-kindly.
>
> My shielding this day from ill,
> My shielding this night from harm,
> Ho! ho! both my soul and my body,
> Be by Father, by Son, by Holy Spirit,
> By Father, by Son, by Holy Spirit.
>
> Be the Father shielding me,
> Be the Son shielding me,
> Be the Spirit shielding me,
> As Three and as One:
> Ho! ho! ho! as Three and as One.

There are many herding songs which the men sang as they drove their cows and sheep to pasture. Everyone knew that the King of Shepherds would watch over both men and flocks, as He had always done, to protect them from the many dangers of the hills and bring them safely home. So this was a common refrain when talking to the animals:

> Be the herding of God the Son about your feet,
> Safe and whole may ye home return.

From this wholeness within the self comes a readiness to be open towards the whole universe, and to be receptive to the people and the things of that universe with all the five senses:

>Bless to me, O God,
>>Each thing mine eye sees;
>Bless to me, O God,
>>Each sound mine ear hears;
>Bless to me, O God,
>>Each odour that goes to my nostrils;
>Bless to me, O God,
>>Each taste that goes to my lips,
>>Each note that goes to my song,
>>Each ray that guides my way,
>>Each thing that I pursue,
>>Each lure that tempts my will,
>>The zeal that seeks my living soul,
>The Three that seek my heart,
>>The zeal that seeks my living soul,
>The Three that seek my heart.

In another poem the action takes on a wider significance for the fire becomes symoblic of the flame of love which should be kept burning for the whole family of mankind.

>I will kindle my fire this morning
>In the presence of the holy angels of heaven,
>In the presence of Ariel of the loveliest form,
>In the presence of Uriel of the myriad charms,
>Without malice, without jealousy, without envy,
>Without fear, without terror of anyone under the sun,
>But the Holy Son of God to shield me.
>>Without malice, without jealousy, without envy,
>>Without fear, without terror of anyone under the sun,
>>But the Holy Son of God to shield me.
>God, kindle Thou in my heart within
>A flame of love to my neighbour,
>To my foe, to my friend, to my kindred all,
>To the brave, to the knave, to the thrall,
>O Son of the loveliest Mary,
>From the lowliest thing that liveth,
>To the Name that is highest of all.

The following poem is believed to be composed by Columba on the occasion of his pleading before Aedh, monarch of Ireland, to free Aidan, king of the Albanian Scots from the tribute long imposed upon his people. When the Irish monarch refused to remit that galling tribute imposed upon the Irish who colonized a portion of Alba or Scotland, the saint arose, and before the king and chiefs assembled, foretold the downfall of Tara, then the most magnificent seat of royalty in Europe. His address had the desired effect. Some centuries after this, Tara was cursed by St. Ruadan, and was therefore abandoned, so that, according to the prophecy, Tara was no more the seat of a king or chief.

Tara of Magh Bregia which you now see so prosperous,
Shall be covered with grass - all its buildings as well as its elevated site,
It shall not be long ere it becomes a desert,
Though it is today in the enjoyment of prosperous affluence!

I assure you in serious verity,
O Tara, the flourishing seat of monarchy,
That there is not to-night on the wide expanse of Banba
A place, alas! fated to enjoy such brief stability.

The repulsive denials there met from day to day,
Strongly excite my charitable complement;
Prosperity will forsake its hills,
In consequence of the rudeness and inhospitality that there prevails.

To a place where neither people nor dwellings are found
None will resort to solicit a favour;
Sorrow must await those who make bad use of their means,
And share not with the necessitous.

Woe betide those who practise repulsiveness and refusals
Who repel the peasant and the prince alike,
It is the penalty which the acts of princes earned,
That Tara shall be devoid of a house for ever.

Oileach and Tara, now seats of power,
Rath-cruachin, and Eamhain the lofty;
Shall be deserted, though now so replenished,
To such an extent that a roof-tree shall not remain on the raths.

The chief cause of this downfall shall be –
As the King of Kings hath assured to me –
Because the chiefs of Ireland of the slender towers,
Do not believe in CHRIST without hesitation.

It shall not so happen to the saints,
Who are in compact with Him of the benign countenance
The joys prepared for them will increase each day,
In Heaven without any deception.

I assure you, without fear of contradiction –
For I have the information from my Heavenly King –
That no one shall find either a king or prince,
Or obtain food or drink within the walls of Tara.

Bed prayers which bring the day to its close reflect sleep and death in terms of the continuing presence of God and the angels. These poems speak vividly, tenderly and securely of what their presence means.

> I lie in my bed
> As I would lie in the grave,
> Thine arm beneath my neck,
> > Thou Son of Mary victorious.
>
> Angles shall watch me
> And I lying in slumber,
> And angels shall guard me
> > In the sleep of the grave.
>
> Uriel shall be at my feet,
> Ariel shall be at my back,
> Gabriel shall be at my head,
> > And Raphael shall be at my side.
>
> Michael shall be with my soul,
> The strong shield of my love!
> And the Physician Son of Mary
> Shall put the salve to mine eye,
> > The Physician Son of Mary
> > Shall put the salve to mine eye!

And if by chance that night's sleep should turn into the death-sleep, then God's arm will still be there:

> Be it that on Thine own arm,
> O God of Grace, that I in peace shall waken.

LINES WRITTEN TO A BOY WHO ASKED

"WHAT WAS ST. COLUMBA LIKE?"

Do you suppose Columba,
When he came to Isle of Hy,
Was a gloomy sort of misery
With looks devoid of glee;
To make you feel all "goupy"
And afraid to make a jest?
So modern books would have it,
Yet I think that book is best
Which shows him as he really was,
A Prince of royal blood
Who once had fought with targe and sword,
Until he saw the Rood.
Then, with a gallant purpose,
Letting fall the sword of hate,
He entered on that joyous war
Whose end is heaven's gate.

He left his targe and claymore
Where Irish waters foam:
He left his father's palace
To build his Father's home.

He built it not of ivory,
But of wattle grass and rod,
And the only armour left him
Was the panoply of God.
His Bible – which he once had kept
Beneath his soldier's kit –
Became his foremost weapon:
For he found the Word would fit
Far closer than a coat of mail,
To defy the fiercest dart
The Devil could let fly at him
(Which is the Devil's part).

He who once fed on venison,
On fat tame geese of 'Derry,
And drank the spacious wines of France,
Now feasted on the berry,
On carrageen – from seaweed made –
And Camus-netted fishes,
And drank the cold spring water
Drawn up in wicker dishes.
(You can see the spring to-day there
With the wicker for the dishes;
Even now you sometimes eat
Of Camus-netted fishes.)
Yet still it was a richer fare
Than 'Derry courts had given,
For crowning every Sabbath
Was the food that came from heaven.
The strong rich bread from far Tiree
And wine from heather blending
That consecrated hearts had made
The feast – that hath no ending –
But still is ours (as is that spring
Beneath its common board),
For our taking or our passing,
The gift of the living Lord.

Thus did the young Columba,
And all within his fold,
Find the greatest jest of history,
The jest that's never old –
That it's folk who "don't want nothing"
Find the whole world is their "room";
The sea responds to "ducks and drakes";
And laughter softens labours;
All the birds are feathered friends:
And sun and storm are neighbours:
Dirges die and dances start;
An end to "bated breath" –
Why! when Love becomes your partner
You can even smile at Death.

G. F. MacLeod

CONCLUSION

My book is ended, but the memories of Iona, a pink rock set in a sapphire sea girt with silver sands, will never end. I close my eyes and hear the continuous breathing of the winds and waves, deeper and more prolonged on the west where the open sea is, but audible everywhere. I hear the incessant chatter and call of the sea-fowls; the gannets and guillemots, skuas and herring-gulls, the long-necked northern diver, the tern, and the cormorant.

I can see the dazzling whiteness of the sand over the north end of the island and the indescribable translucent green sea as it washes over the shore. I recall the scent of the wild-flowers among the craigs and moorlands: the bloom of the heather, the belts of yellow iris gleaming among the meadows, the king-cups covering the marshy ground with a golden carpet, the little yellow St. John's Wort growing in wild profusion in the damp shady corners, the buttercups, daisies, thyme and clover.

I hear the bleating of the lambs and ewes coming up the slope of Dun I from the Machair that lies between its west slope and the shoreless sea to the west. I see the twelve adventurous monks in their small sea-tossed coracles landing on that rough wave-swept bay and then scrambling up the slope of the Cairn of-the-back-to-Erin to satisfy themselves that Ireland could not be seen from the island.

I hear the vesters sung by hooded monks praising the Lord in a strange land – brave monks that forfeited their lives at the hands of pirates to keep the flame of Truth alive. The hutments of Columba and his followers are gone, but the beauty of the sea and sky of Iona are as they were many hundreds of years ago when Columba chose Iona as a place apart from the world – in the world but out of it.

I remember having dinner one evening at the home of Dr. George MacLeod (in Edinburgh), the founder of the Iona Community. This community was given the Abbey as their center by the Church of Scotland. When I expressed a desire to write a book on Iona for American readers, it was Dr. MacLeod's encouragement and permission to excerpt from the publications of the Community that gave birth to my story of Iona.

I can tell the story of the history of Iona, but to tell its spirit I cannot match the words of Fione MacLeod:

"In spiritual geography Iona is the Mecca of the Gael, a small island, fashioned of a little sand, a few grasses salted with the spray of an ever restless wave, a few rocks that wade in heather and upon whose brows the sea-wind weaves the yellow lichen. But since remotest days sacrosanct men have bowed here in worship.

"In this little island was lit a lamp whose flame lighted pagan Europe from the Saxon in his fen to the swarthy folk who came by Greek waters to trade the Orient. Here Learning and Faith had their tranquil home. From age to age lowly hearts have never ceased to bring their burdens here. Iona herself has given us for remembrance a fount of youth more wonderful than that which lies under her own boulders of Dun I. And here hope waits . . . ."

• • • • • •

I see the fulfillment of Columba's prophecy of the years of desolation that would befall Iona and its restoration:

> "In Iona of my heart, Iona of my love,
> Instead of monk's voices shall be lowing of cattle.
> But ere the world come to an end
> Iona shall be as it was."

I'll never forget an old fisherman's last words as I ended my first visit to Iona and boarded a small boat for the mainland. "Hoch! not goodby, mon, for we say on the island that if ye come once, ye'll come thrice more before ye dee!"

Janice and I did return twice more before she fell alseep in Jesus.

The End

E° Raymond Copt

NOTABLE DATES IN THE HISTORY OF IONA

200-250 Iona divided between Picts of Alban and Irish King Riada

563 St. Columba lands on Iona

597 Death of St. Columba

679 Adamnan (biographer of Columba) installed as Abbot

794-795 First Viking raid on Iona

801 Abbey destroyed by Norse pirates

806 Sixty-eight monks killed by Vikings at Martyrs' Bay Columba's shrine moved to Kells in Ireland

825 Abbot Blaithmac killed by pirates

986 Norse pirates plunder Iona killing Abbot and fifteen monks

1074 Iona Monastery restored by Queen Margaret

1203 Benedictine Abbey founded

1204 Last of Columban monks leaving Iona

1266 Norway cedes Western Isles (including Iona) to Scotland

1500 Abbey of Iona made a Cathedral Church

1561 Iona Abbey dismantled after the Reformation

1574 Mackay of Duart seizes Iona

1688 Earl of Argyll takes Iona

1690 Presbyterian re-established

1695 Clan Campbell (Dukes of Argyll) take control of Iona

1840 Iona Parish Church built on Iona

1899 Iona Abbey given to Church of Scotland by eight Duke of Argyll

1910 Iona Cathedral restored by Duke of Argyll

1938 Restoration of Abbey ruins begun by Iona Community

1979 Major part of Iona gifted to National Trust for Scotland

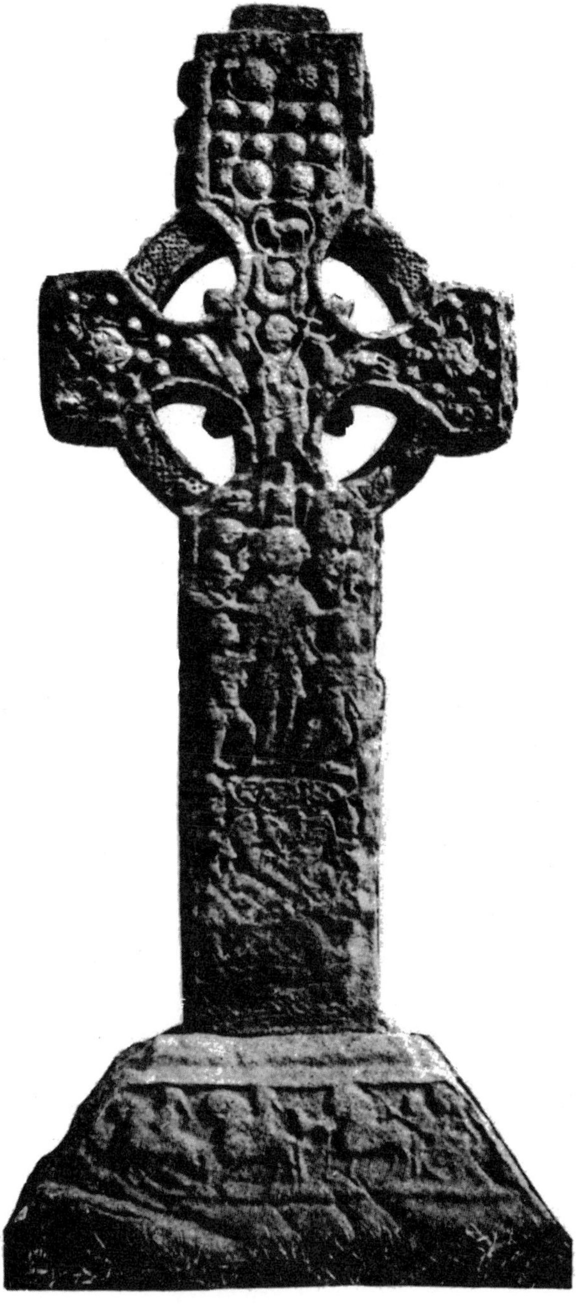

SYMBOLS OF THE FOUR EVANGELISTS
BOOK OF KELLS

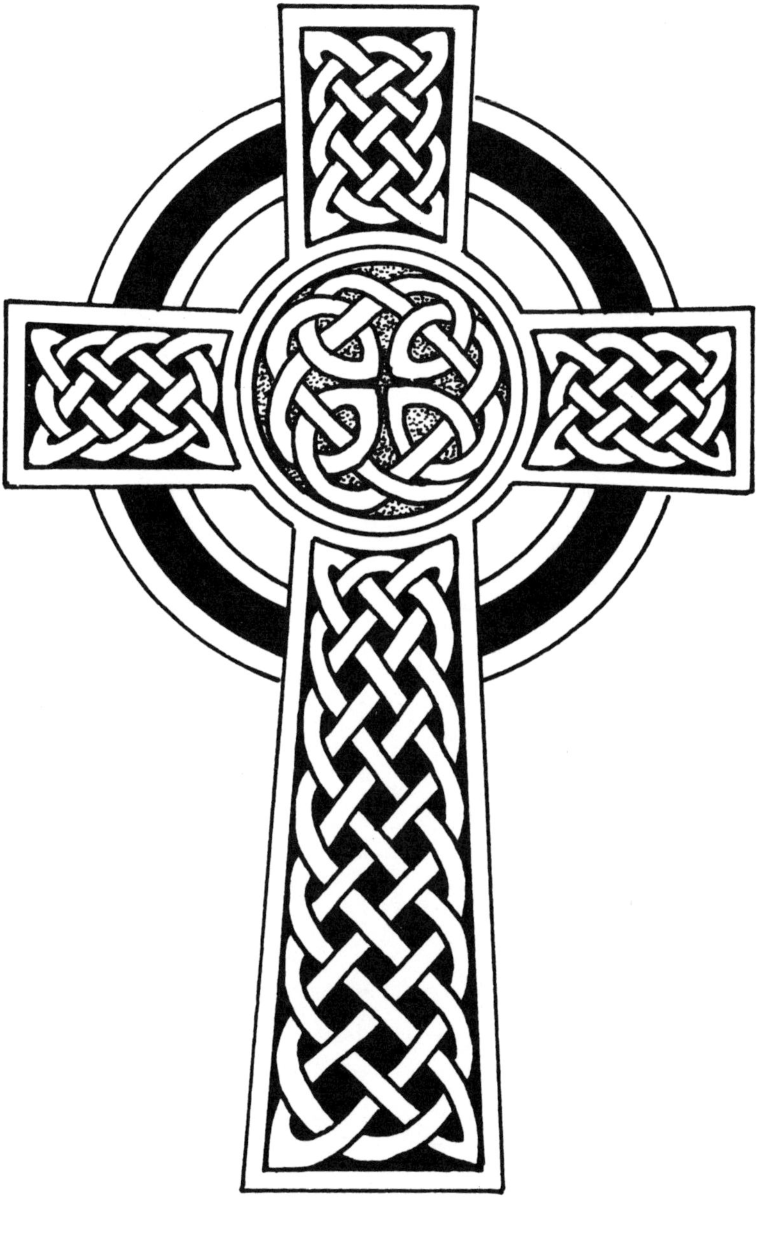

Pictures of Iona

Heather

Nunnery Gardens

Hebridean Landscape - Machair

Ruins of Bee-Hive Huts

Columba's Bee-Hive Hut Ruins

White Strand of the Monks

Ruins of Columba's Cell

Columba's Bay

St. Martin's Caves

Dun I

Rock Caverns

Port Ban

Marble Quarry

Archean Rocks

Looking East of Iona
Mull in distance

Rocky East Coast of Iona

Looking West of Iona

Looking North of Iona

Looking Northwest of Iona
Treshnish Island of Staffa in distance

East Wall Choir Window

South Transcept Celtic Window

Communion Tables of Iona Marble

Effigy of Abbot Mackenzie

Effigy of George Dovglas Campbell and his wife

Restored Cloisters

Nave of St. Mary's Cathedral

Choir of St. Mary's Cathedral

Tor Abb

Iona Abbey and Cathedral

Nunnery Ruins

Graveyard of the Kings

Michael Chapel

Descent of the Spirit

Abbey Well

Graveyard of the Kings

Grave Slabs in Museum

St. Columba's Shrine behind St. John's Cross

Entrance to the Nave of Abbey

The author and his wife